Truth

OLIVIA LOUCKS

Truth

KNOWING **TRUE LOVE** IN THE LORDS TRUTH

Charleston, SC
www.PalmettoPublishing.com

Truth

Copyright © 2021 by Olivia Loucks

All rights reserved

First Edition

Paperback ISBN: 978-1-63837-719-1

Intro

Are we truly realizing the life we are living? The meaning of life is so much more than we think. Once we realize the true meaning of life, we live and truly enjoy each day knowing each day is all we have. When you have been through many flaming fires in life, knowing that you have succeeded in making positive changes in your life, you begin to see life as the Lord created it to be which is good. If you're struggling to fight your flaming fires in life that's ok too. In life, we all bare some kind of cross the Lord allows us to have. You climb that mountain so you can see the beautiful view on the other side. Our crosses in life build our character into the person the Lord knows we can be. Jeremiah 29:11 "For I know the plans I have for you, declares the Lord, plans to prosper you and not to harm you, plans to give you hope and a future."

Annabelle Frank was a very intuitive young lady. She never seemed to fit in with any kind of groups in school. She was constantly bullied for being timid and shy. She never liked confrontation, so she had so much emotional and mental anger built up inside. There were points where Annabelle would hide away in her room and put her ear phones into her iPod blasting the volume on high. It was her way of running away from her hurt and truth from the real world as nothing seemed to truly mend her emotional pain. She felt like no one understood her and she didn't truly understand herself. The

Lord knew Annabelle though. He knew who he created her to be which is radiant and pure of heart. He laid into her gifts she would soon come to understand to not only help herself, but others as well.

Living in a world full of evil and good, God allows us to face challenges and experience low points in our lives, helping us to grow into his image and to be who we were truly created to be. Having free will allows sin and with sin, we are all equal to one another. The only difference is our gifts, talents and personalities. The Lord created us unique in that aspect. Can you imagine not going through any challenges in life? What kind of character would we have? Who would we be?

One of the apostles from the Bible named Paul had his own share of difficulties similar to Annabelle. Paul's name was Saul before he became Paul and he persecuted many Christians. God opened Paul's heart and understanding when he blinded his sight. Paul, in his blindness, was truly awakened to the truth of God's word. He repented his ways and then lived on for Christ. It wasn't easy for him as many people went against him. He even went to jail for quite some time, but the amazing truth to this story is that God can change anyone. No matter who we are, we can be a vessel for the Lord in his work. We can be the hands and feet of Jesus. Paul went on to write about his story and how God had changed him for the better. He also composed many parts of the Bible, even while he was in jail behind bars. God created and knows each and every one of us. He hand crafted us all differently, but we are all in his image. God is an almighty perfect being and when we choose to look up to Jesus and follow in his footsteps, instead of mankind, we will experience more happiness and light in our lives.

Chapter 1

G rowing up in the mile-high city, in Denver Colorado was an adventure for my family and I (Annabelle). We didn't do much moving around, but there was always a lot to explore. Whether it was the hustle and bustle of the city life or the serenity of the peaceful mountains, you were never truly bored. As a child, my parents did everything they could for my younger brother and I. They gave us opportunity and always took care of us. My mom would stay home with us while my dad worked full time for an oil and gas company. He would wake up early every morning and go to work down town into the city. We lived in the suburbs so it was about a 20-to-30-minute drive to the city. My dad would take his car down to the bus station, so he wouldn't have to pay for parking. It was extremely expensive downtown. My parents always taught me hard work pays off. Its hard work to raise children and hard work to work a job. No matter what you do in life, always give one hundred and ten percent. Lazy was not an option in our home.

Babies are born pure, needing lots of love and attention. As children they continue to need lots love and attention and want to be loved for who they are. Of course, not only children but adults can feel this way too. Sometimes, as adults we lose that initial love, depending on what kind of experiences we go through. Luckily, Jesus is the ultimate love even when all else on earth fails. John 3:16 "For God so loved the world that he gave his only son, that whoever believes in him shall not parish, but have everlasting life."

From the time I was two to six years old, we lived in a suburban neighborhood by the church. It was nice because we didn't have to drive very far to get to and from church or even schools. I remember a lot from growing up in that house. We had many days at the park where my dad would play froggy with us. He would chase us around and hop like a frog pretending to get us. After prayer for bed time, we would also play horse. He would go on his hands and knees and he would give us rides on his back galloping around. My mom would always say, "Be careful kids! Don't hurt your dad."

The church we went to and still attend is The New Apostolic Church. You don't really hear many of these kinds of churches now a days. It's not Catholic but it does descend from one of the catholic branches. It's pretty much a Christian based church. One of the reasons I love this church is not because of religion, but because its unique. It's not like other churches or religions where the Bible may be confusing and have a bunch of abolishing rules. Here everyone is accepted and the Bible is factual. They have service for the departed to remember and honor those who have died or need help in eternity. We take the time for holy communion and remembrance. Church is never perfect, like a hospital filled with sick people. The only reason people come to church is to be with other sinners who all come together to worship and get to know and love our God, Jesus and Holy Spirit. It is truly 100% all about your one-on-one relationship with God, Jesus and Holy Spirit. They want to know you and become your best friend. That's what it's all about.

My parents and their parents both attended the church. My mother's parents Harold and Karen met each other in Michigan as neighbors. They grew up playing together and became the best of friends. One day my grandpa just asked my grandma on a date and it went off from there. They attended the Lutheran church for a while until they stumbled across the church we go to now. My grandparents moved all over the place with my mom and her older brother because of my grandmas Fibromyalgia condition. It was hard to find medical answers for that illness back then so they did what they could and moved until they found a solution. My grandpa had to start his business three times because of the moves, but God always provided for them. My grandpa owned his own shutter and awning business. He worked so hard in that business and also worked very hard as a Priest in the church. He worked hard to help people and offer them work even though he could barely afford anything himself. He helped build the church in the neighborhood I lived in. He always gave God everything he had.

My dad's parents lived in Texas growing up. David and Margie met each other in Ohio through a mutual friend. They had burger's together in high school on a double date with some friends and they hit it off ever sense. Throughout some time when my dad and his younger brother were little kids, they lived in Ohio for quite some time. David got a job promotion later on in life and moved the family out to Texas. My dad's parents came across the church back in Ohio when my dad and his brother were younger. The New Apostolic Church is actually a world-wide church. It's amazing because no matter where you may live in the world, there is a church. My grandpa was an amazing person and Priest in the church. Him and my grandma were the experts at garage sales. They always found everything needed and it always amazed me that no matter what, they could always find something amazing. Even at church my grandparents would always find things for others and help them in any way they could. It was the true meaning of Christ and his love.

In the last detail of my stories time line, my parents met in the youth group. Our church would have huge events to get all of the youth from all around the world together. We would call it day of the youth. That's when our Chief Apostle would come out to hold service and everyone would get together and have a blast playing games and etc. My parents met each other when they had day of the youth in Texas. They talked and met briefly at that time, but also didn't really know one another. After the day of the youth, my dad began to write my mom thinking about her often. One day he finally came out to Colorado where she was living and that was the end of it.

Living in the first home on Brewer Street we had for the first couple of years was fun. My parents had my younger brother and we would constantly play together. We did have our fights of course, but it was like any other childhood. I'll always remember my parents taking the time to play with us or spend time with us. They always made us a priority and took care of our needs. When I was around four years of age, I remember having a wide range of imagination. I always felt the presence of God around me or eternity. I remember praying to myself often and looking at the world from a child's perspective. I prayed to God by myself many nights to pray for eternity and the people around me in my life. One night I prayed, "Lord, I want to help heal people. I wish I could help the people in the hospitals or people in pain. It's not fair." I got very emotional and began to cry. I could feel the nearness of God and a quiet voice saying, "Do you want to help people Olivia?" I replied, "Yes."

I had a hard time growing up at times. I didn't feel like a normal little kid. I felt something was off with myself because I was more sensitive than all the other kids. I could feel my emotions like a roller coaster ride. I felt very invisible because of how shy I was compared to other kids. I was very introverted. In preschool we had times where we would sing songs together and jump or run around and scream. I'll never forget hating the screaming. I felt as if I didn't belong as a kid with all the energy and screaming, they all had. I had one close friend that I got along with well at the time named Peggy. Peggy was always nice to me. She got along with everyone pretty well and was a likable person. Peggy's brother was also around my younger brothers age, so they went to the same preschool and grew up together as well. Our families became the best of friends. We would even spend some of the holidays together. I still felt like I was not sure of why I still didn't fit in as well. My question to myself as I grew up was, why don't I fit in or where do I fit in?

Chapter 2

W hen I got into the second grade, I was nearly seven years old. We moved into our new house on Hallway Street. It was much bigger than the house we had on Brewer Street. We had a park across the way so it was easy to be able to play many different kinds of sports or games. My brother and I went to the Elementary school that was in the neighborhood. It was a hard transition at first because I had a good friend named Brianna that I didn't want to leave back at the old school. It was hard for me to make any new friends from being so timid.

I will never forget my first day in the second grade. I felt panic attacks constantly and felt like I could feel everyone in the room on a high vibration. I didn't know what anxiety was at the time being so young. All I knew how to do was freak out and cry. I would have many constant melt downs every time I had to go to gym. Something about that teacher made me feel sicker with anxiety than I ever felt in the classroom. My teacher was a very kind lady. She was older, but didn't understand my anxiety. Every time I had gym; I would get physically ill from the anxiety it caused me to be around that specific teacher. It got to the point of where my second-grade teacher would say, "Mr. Smart is a nice teacher. He's like a teddy bear, there is nothing to be afraid of." I was embarrassed of my out busts and crying in front of everyone. I felt completely off from everyone else.

People would tease me as time went on. I was known as the loser who no one really wanted to sit with. I felt like I had no control over my emotions. I would just mostly internalize them and try to fit in and be accepted. My parents didn't know what was going on with me either at the time. They thought it could be related to diet or something.

At age ten, I was starting to transition from child to teenager. I had an amazing fourth grade teacher who was so kind, patience and friendly with everyone. She really knew how to teach a class well and help everyone in their own way. Everyone has a different way to learn things, so it was nice to have different analogies. It wasn't like middle school yet where one would have many teachers in the year; We just had one in Elementary school.

My parents liked to take us on hikes many times throughout the summer to enjoy the mountains when I was in Elementary school. At the time I didn't really like hiking much, but I knew they liked it. We went on this hike once where it was a little more uphill than I was used to. There was no railing around us and we had to take steps very carefully. I was upset because I didn't like it very much without the railing or some kind of support. As I was trying to tell my parents that maybe we should turn back, I started tripping over myself. I fell to my knees on the cliff we were on and started to roll down the hill very quickly. My Dad and Mom freaked out. My Dad tried to get to me as quickly as possible as I was tumbling for death down the cliff. All of the sudden I stopped rolling. I felt an unknown force like an angel stand in the way suddenly. My Dad didn't get to me quick enough, but I was stopped with nothing physically in front of me. Once, my Dad got to me I was thankful to God. I thought at that point I was a goner.

Eternity for me was very real because of all of these testimonies of faith.

Back then we had church services every Sunday and Wednesday. Sundays were at 10:30am and Wednesdays were at 7:30pm. At the time my dad was a Priest in the church so he had many meetings and things to go to other than church itself. Both of my grandpas were also Priests in the church as well. One night as my mom was cleaning up dinner before our evening church service, I decided to play the piano for a while. I was just playing around with different tunes when suddenly, I felt and saw someone sitting next to me in the chair by the piano. It was unreal for me. The little boy sitting next to me had chestnut brown hair like my mom and had crystal blue eyes like my dad. I looked to him and said, "Who are you?" He didn't reply. Instead, he smiled and followed me into the kitchen where my mom was finishing up the dishes. I sat on our bench near the garage door puzzled. As I looked up, I saw the little boy reach out his hands with tears streaming down his face to my mom saying, "Mom, I love you." He looked over to me and replied, "My name is Andy."

Astonished I waved at my mom and said, "Mom, I need to ask you something." She turned around ready to listen. "I see a little boy here with brown hair and blue eyes." I went on to explain how the little boy reached out his hands to my mom calling her mom and how much he loved her. "His name is Andy." I spoke. She shook her head in disbelief. "Olivia, how could you have known that I had a miscarriage a couple of years ago? We named him Andy." My mom was shocked at the time but didn't think anything of it. She thought it was just a moment in time where God allowed me to have a vision of some sort. What she was about to realize is how it wasn't just a faze or a moment with a vision, it was my life.

Going into middle school was like going from collected to chaos. I never realized how peaceful and quiet my elementary school was until I walked in the halls of my middle school. Kids were disrespectful to other kids and teachers. There was more freedom than in elementary school, but more chaos. People would be running into other people on purpose with back packs and school books. Even teachers would get pushed aside. There were no boundaries and no limits. It was something I was not use to. There were many bullies around and seldom nice kids. It was a war zone of immaturity.

The only class I loved in middle school was orchestra. When I saw the orchestra playing for the first time, I knew I wanted to play an instrument. I loved the way the instruments all played different parts and played beautifully together as one. For some reason, God gave me a gift to be able to read music and play fairly well on the Violin. I got many awards throughout middle school including directors award. To me it's not about the awards; it's about using our gifts for the Lord. He created us and our gifts so really, it's all him. I was grateful for the opportunity to play in the orchestra with everyone. It's truly an amazing experience.

My Great Grandpa died when I was in sixth grade. It was hard for my Dad and his side of the family most of all because it was his grandpa. He loved and cared for his family very much. A week later, I had a dream about Great Grandpa. In the dream, I was with my Great Grandma at the airport. We were getting ready to board the plane to leave when Great Grandpa came up wanting to join us. I told him that he couldn't go with us because he had passed away and was now in eternity. I knew it was hard for him to let go because of how much he wanted to be with my Great Grandma. He was hurting and upset. Sometimes it is hard for people who have recently passed to move forward in eternity. It's a new chapter for them in the next eternal life. I woke up the next morning after the dream and asked the Lord to help him. To have angels be by his side to help him in crossing over. There are many different kinds of realms you can go to once you pass on. Depending on what kind of life you chose to live is where you go until Jesus comes back.

Throughout middle school we got some unfortunate news that my Mom had an illness called Chronic Fatigue Syndrome. It's an illness that comes from a mono strain, and can make you feel like you have mono for years. One may have so many different things with this illness; sometimes it can go undiagnosed. My Mom had this illness so bad that she had to stay in bed for a year and a half. I can't imagine the pain of what she had to go through. She was a true trooper. The illness was also hard on my brother and I let alone my Dad. It was hard for us all to see her this way. I started acting out in school getting in trouble a lot and my brother was sad a lot. We all had to pitch in a lot more because my Mom couldn't. I was a hard time for everyone. We just wanted her to get better.

We tried getting some pets for comfort such as a rabbit and a dog. Our rabbits name was Thumper; sometimes we would call him Juju. He was a very lovable bunny and was truly hilarious. I loved to cuddle with him on my stomach. He would hop around all over the couch and jump off back into his cage. In the winters, he would love being thrown off the deck and into the snow. He would hop right back to us to be thrown back into the snow. When spring and summer hit, we would let him run around outside in the backyard. He would hop around and dig under the fence. Many times, our neighbors found him at the park across the street.

The dog we had was another story. Before we got Thumper, we got a dog named Golden. She was a mix between Shepard and Collie. She was the friendliest dog I ever met. We had to keep her outside most of the time because she would tear up the interior of the house. First getting her was exciting. It was our very first pet that we ever had. She was such a playful and energetic dog that it got to a bad point. She would be sneaky and hop the fence! Our fencing was fairly tall. It was made of long cedar wood that would go up many feet. It truly shocked us when she could jump over these huge fences. She knew everyone in our neighborhood from jumping the fence. We got constant phone calls that someone had our dog. At one point we had to give Golden back to the shelter because it was just too much for us to keep up with. She really needed a farm or lots of land to run around in.

In middle school I really didn't fit in anywhere just like elementary school. At least in middle school I did have some friends. I was still an outcast. In seventh and eighth grade near the end of my time in middle school, I started to get crushes. I had a crush on these two guys that I liked for quite some time. I finally had the courage to tell them at one point during the school year and I got made fun of for it from them. It was a challenge to not only be made fun of by one person, but two. I was also bullied very badly throughout that time from a girl whose name was my name. Apparently, she did not like that so she had to bully me constantly. I didn't do anything about the bulling. I just took it with a grain of salt most of the time. Other times I would cry my way home from the emotional and verbal abuse. Her friends and her would gang up on me as I would shrivel back into my internal shell. There were times that they would try to throw rocks at me as well.

In eighth grade I truly started falling in love with the Lord. We tried going to a non-denominational church for a while as a family. It was slightly different from the New Apostolic Church. At this church they had huge rock bands that would play for service every Sunday. They were so big that they had three church services. I wasn't use to the rock bands and the complete openness of worship. It truly helped me personally open up and help me in my relationship with the Lord. There were tons of people and kids that went to this church it felt like a concert. There were so many activities and youth groups it was crazy to me. At the New Apostolic Church, it was more old school. We sang songs from Hymnals and had a choir as well. We weren't big enough yet to have an actual band, but it was still very different. At first, I didn't want to attend this new church, but the Lord knew I needed it for what was to come.

Chapter 3

Highschool was more mature than middle school. People actually had more boundaries with each other. They wouldn't ram into other people with their books or back packs. Most people were actually pretty respectful. It was a breath of fresh air for me compared to middle school. Middle school was like a bad repeat of a war zone. My favorite class was still orchestra. I loved playing with everyone and learning new music pieces.

In the beginning of nineth grade, I started to feel a bit different than I normally was. I started feeling extremely worn down and tired all the time. I also started having many panic attacks and constant anxiety. I felt as if I was coming down with a bug constantly. It was alarming to me and I wanted to figure out what was going on. My mom thought I might have gotten what she had which was Chronic Fatigue Syndrome, but it wasn't. I went to the doctors for help and I started my journey with eating healthier. I was even put on some anxiety and depression medication to help. There were points in time where I couldn't even walk around the block of our neighborhood without getting anxious. It was extremely strange to me. Eventually I had to drop out of high school because it had gotten so bad. I couldn't attend classes normally like everyone else. I had some extreme issues.

Along with my physical and emotional issues, I was starting to really see and feel energy all around me. It was like a light bulb went off and everything turned on. I could feel everything from everyone. If someone was upset with anger or sadness, I could feel their emotions and see the colors around them. If I was in a big group of people like the classroom or youth group, my anxiety would go sky high because I would feel everyone's space. There were many people concerned about me including some friends, family and youth group. They didn't understand what was going on with me, but all I knew is that the Lord opened a door to the unknown.

As I stayed home in the winter months being a high school dropout, I started to regain strength. I was feeling good trying to heal my body and emotional anxiety. During spring at the end of March, a lot of things started to happen to me. My Dad and younger brother were in Texas at the time for spring break and my Mom was in her room trying to recover from the store. She was still trying to recover from Chronic Fatigue Syndrome. She had her ups and downs with her energy levels so she had to pace herself. This spring break was harder for her and was feeling truly emotionally down from the trauma of the illness.

After our rabbit we had when I was in elementary school, we got a little chiweenie and named her Missy when I got into high school. She was the sweetest little dog. I treated her like my little baby. She loved car rides and loved going to Mc Donald's for her annual vanilla ice cream cone. She was spoiled and very loved.

I took Missy out on a walk that day on spring break while my Mom was trying to cope with her illness. For some reason, I just felt like I needed to go on this walk. Suddenly, I felt a huge sense of comfort and joy I couldn't explain come over me. All of the sudden a presence was standing with me. The man was dressed in pure white clothing. He had dark chocolate brown hair and eyes. His skin literally radiated light brighter than a burning candle. He had holes in his hands and feet. Also, a scar on his side. At that moment I knew who he was; He was Jesus the Messiah. I started bawling my eyes out and bowing my head in honor right outside our house. He said to me, "Olivia, let's go for a walk together." His voice was gentle and his presence was humbling. I couldn't believe what was happening; I was in complete shock.

As we walked together, he started talking with me telling me things I needed to hear and know with words of wisdom. He said, "If you struggle, if you ask God to heal you and ask for the things you want and it doesn't happen, tell yourself that you have lived the Lord's plan for me. Not the things that I have wanted, but the things that God has wanted. The things I needed not wanted. The change for a new beginning, a new start, eternity." This was the very first time I had ever felt and seen Jesus like this. It was the best blessing and experience I could have ever asked for in my life.

After the walk with Jesus, I went into the house and up to my mom where she was suffering. She was having a really rough time with her chronic illness. She felt like giving up. I told her what had happened outside with seeing Jesus for the first time. I told her what Jesus said to me and how he also wanted to say this to her, especially in her time of need and comfort. She cried and said, "This is exactly what I needed today. I felt like giving up." She was amazed at what I was telling her. It was like a dream, but it wasn't. Deuteronomy 31:6 "Be strong and courageous. Do not be afraid or terrified because of them, for the Lord your God goes with you; he will never leave you nor forsake you."

Once April hit, I went to my mom's therapists' house. At her house my Mom and I would talk and try to figure out what was going on with me. The therapist was a natural path person. She liked physic stuff and believed anyone could see and feel even without being given the gift from God. It is like saying, I believe that anyone can be a doctor, even if they aren't given that talent of gift from God. Everyone was made unique and different. Not everyone is meant to be a doctor and that is good. We need people with different gifts and different specialties to be able to function in this world. You would not want to put yourself in harm's way trying to make yourself have a gift that you don't have. Especially when it comes to eternity and that vale. It's not a joke or a game to be played with. It's an actual world where you have to understand and respect it.

As we were continuing our session, a man named Jack knocked on our therapist's door. He came in and introduced himself as an energy healer. He explained that an energy healer is someone that helps another person clear out bad and negative energy. The energy healer balances out the body and helps the person move on, let go, heal from illness and disease, and etc. Energy healers do many things if God has called you to this calling and if you happen to have that kind of gift to see and feel things. Sometimes people may call energy healers hands of light. It reminds me of how Jesus would heal the blind and the sick with just a touch, I know we are nothing compared to Jesus, but energy healers do similar work in that perspective.

Jack took us through all kinds of energy healing practices, but they were completely incorrect. He stated that to calm our energy and nervous system that my Mom and I had to put our feet together while lying on the ground and picture our energy running through each other. This practice is completely incorrect because running two separate energies together creates chaos. We are separate beings and created that way from God. There is never ever a time where we need to use each other's energy supply for our own. We get our energy and who we are in creation by the Lord. Our energy supply to let go and function comes from earth energy and cosmic energy that the Lord himself created. We are not just physically created from the dirt of the earth; we are also created from energy both earth and cosmic to be able to have a soul.

We have seven charkas that the Lord created us with. The root chakra is found at the base of the spine. This is the foundation of who we are and how we built our life. It represents security and stability. Also, the color is red. The sacral chakra is found at an inch below the naval. It represents our sexuality and creativity. The color for this is orange. Solar plexus is the third charka. Its located under the chest on the gut. This represents will power, decision making, and self-esteem. The color for this is yellow. The fourth charka is the heart. Its color is green and indicates relationships and self-love. This is located in the middle of the chest. Blue is the color that radiates from the fifth throat charka. This is located under the chin on the throat. It represents speaking clearly. The third eye or the sixth charka is a really powerful charka. It indicates intuition, clarity and fore sight. The color dark purple comes from this and is located between the eye brows on the fore head. The crown is the last charka located on the top of the head. The color that comes from this is a light purple. It represents divine connection like prayer, worship and connection to the Lord.

We may have blockages in our charkas throughout life that can cause problems down the road. It can occur in physical pain or even internally with mental and emotional trauma. That's why the Lord created meditation to look inward within ourselves. To see why we stand in our own way at times with our baggage or things we need to let go of. Allowing God to heal us from within. Lastly, the Lord created what we call the aura. We all have our own little bubble that we have. It is also a part of who we are and may vary in all kinds of different colors. It's our own little space.

Once summer hit in the month of May, more things seemed to be happening in eternity. My Mom went to go see an old friend of ours named Kayla one day for a massage. She owned her own business and worked through her home. She helped many people with a lot of issues with back problems and so on. As the appointment went on that day, my mom felt inclined to say something. "Kayla, have you ever heard of energy healings?" Kayla laughed and said, "Are you talking about your daughter?" My mom sat up and looked at her. "How did you know?" Kayla went on to talk about how she knew I could see and feel things ever sense I was a little girl. She never said anything to my Mom because she was afraid of how she would react. Kayla also had the gift to be able to see and feel things so she could tell when someone else was gifted as well. My Mom was shocked and amazed.

After my Mom had her appointment with Kayla, she came home and told me all about what Kayla had said. Everything was now adding up to why I was so different. I went to my appointment the following week with Kayla. We talked forever it seemed like about eternity and different things we both saw. We shared our experiences and I felt like I finally fit in somewhere. During my appointment with Kayla, my brother Andy showed up again from eternity. He came to show his love and support; that I wasn't alone in this gift. Eternity is so different from our world. No one can understand it fully until we actually pass on and are put into that world.

The next person that came into the room from eternity was arch angel Michael. He was nine feet tall like all the other angels. He wore a white robe outfit with golden belts and swords. His blue eyes were as blue as the oceans in Hawaii and his hair was long and blond. In his kind voice he told me that he was here for me. I couldn't believe that the arch angel Michael was actually there and in the room with me. I felt very blessed and humbled that he would take the time out to talk with me. It was truly indescribable.

At this time, Peggy and I were still good friends with one another. We had a falling out in the end of middle school and beginning of high school and didn't speak to one another anymore. Peggy at the time we were still friends called me one day after she got out of gymnastic practice. She was really upset because she lost her phone. She knew she kept it in her locker and it never moved from there. She didn't want to have to get a new phone when her parents worked so hard. I tried to calm her down over the phone. I started to pray to the Lord and ask him for help or a vision of some sort so I could help her.

At that moment in time, the Lord gave me a vision. I asked her saying, "Hey, was there a basketball team practicing by you all by any chance?" She said, "Yes! Why?" I spoke and said, "Well I believe one of these men stole your phone." I went on and I told her which person it might have been. She was blown away and actually found her phone! I told her to thank the Lord and not me because he was the one giving me the visions. She was thankful and amazed.

That summer was crazy because I learned so much about myself and didn't feel so alone anymore trying to figure out life. I've always been a musician ever sense I started playing the Violin at eleven years old. I took Piano lessons as a child, but truly fell in love with the Violin. There were times where I would sit at the Piano and create worship songs to the Lord. I would also play Worship songs I knew through the radio. In the summer, I decided to sit down and play some Worship songs like I normally would do. In those moments I would feel the presence of God. In those moments I would hear the Lord say, "Annabelle, I don't want you to stop playing. I want you to play for me and show the world my glory." I could feel the Lord and so much more of eternity more than I ever felt in my life.

After attending church one Sunday that summer, I decided to go relax in the basement for a while and watch some tv. Once I got down stairs, I saw a bunch of angels together. Michael the arch angel was there as well and told me that I was going to be a soldier in the battle against evil. I believe that meant serving the Lord in any way I could and being a vessel for him and his work. All of us are true vessels for the Lord. Everyone has different gifts that the Lord has given unto us.

All of the sudden a dark figure appeared across the room. It was not an angel, but also nine feet tall. The man had dark black hair that was short and pure black eyes. His skin looked like it was as white as the cold snow in winter. Pure evil seemed to ring from this man. He spoke to me from the distance smiling a demonic smile. "You will not go through with this." He had been planning this out for centuries. Sense the beginning of time Satan has always tried to harm and destroy mankind. I stood there honestly really freaked out. Satan was standing in my basement. The angels surrounded me as a blue light of energy came up to protect me. The Lord has an amazing light blue energy that is for protection and healing. It is very powerful along with angel's protection. Eventually, Satan vanished and I prayed to the Lord for him to never ever come back.

Chapter 4

E verything is made up of energy. Objects can either have an aura of colors with a grid like appearance, or you just see colors with auras around objects or people. The people who were given the gift to see through the vale of eternity like this are called clairvoyant. I don't like the term medium because medium is like being able to see into the future or do things through spirits. That kind of thing is not of God. It is not the Lord's work. Helping people and being able to rely messages to them from their loved ones is the Lord's work. Also, helping people through something they may not be able to see in their own space.

In July of that summer in ninth grade year, my Mom wanted me to get help with this clairvoyant gift, so she took me to a physic class. She found this through her therapist Kayla. The lady who was holding the class was not being led by God. She was being led by dark spirits at the time. We all got together sitting in chairs with one another waiting to start the class. I felt uneasy the whole time and should have gotten up to leave, but I was still learning. In the class we learned how to clear out our auras of any negative energies which was good. We also learned how to get anyone out of our space in our third eye the sixth charka.

Those were all good things until the lady told us we would have spirits called energy healers that would help us and be with us. Two figures appeared at the time for me. They called themselves Martha and Jesse. I felt really uneasy because I could see Martha's face; she was dark. Jesse was a little easier to see but it was not good. Jesus himself appeared to me in that class near the end and told me to leave and never come back. When dealing with any kind of class like this where they are teaching you about your space and eternity, always go to someone who is faith based. Never go to some person who is being led by a spirit it will hurt you in the long run.

Martha would plug her hands into mine throughout time to start the healing process and help me with my space and energy. Instead, of actually doing this to help me in my space, it was hurting me. She was draining my energy and making me feel down and dark. The same would happen with Jesse as well. Martha was supposed to help with my internal inner self, while Jesse with the actual physical body. After having that negative experience, I felt even more lost. I had no idea what was true and what wasn't. I was lost. Psalm 49:3 "My mouth will speak words of wisdom; the meditation of my heart will give you understanding."

A lady from the New Apostolic church we knew named Mona had the gift to see and feel energies as well. At the time we were still attending the other non-denominational church. We didn't know this until one day we brought our dog Missy over to her for grooming. She owned her own grooming business from her home. Out of the blue, we all started talking about eternity and energies. She didn't have much time to discuss much with us, but wanted to meet up at the park to talk and see if she could try to help me with my gifting.

We met up the following week at the park by both of our homes. It was a good experience compared to the weird physic class. Mona is God centered in her gift. Everything she did and talked about was pure and I didn't feel uneasy about anything with her. She was older compared to me by about 40 years.

She had a lot of wisdom and clarity she offered. She sat down with me on the park bench that day and said, "Can you see the trees auras? How about the people and plants? Everything that God created has a different feeling and frequency." I went over to the tree and she told me to rub my hands together fast for about a minute. She said, "Put your hands now by the tree about an inch away from the tree itself. Your palms facing the tree. What do you feel?" It was amazing. I immediately felt the pine trees energy and how potent it felt on my hands. I could feel the energy of the tree surging. She had me go to another tree that wasn't a pine tree and do the same thing to feel the energy differences. The other oak tree did not have a strong sense of potent energy. It was soft and gentle compared to the pine trees energy. I was shocked and truly amazed at how different energies can feel. She taught me to be a prayer warrior and a peace maker.

Nearing the end of August, I was looking forward to learning online for my tenth-grade year. The one thing I missed from being back in Highschool in person was orchestra. I had a hard time expecting how sensitive I was at times. It was a huge blessing, but it was also a challenge. My frustration was starting to ease at this point, but I still needed help to understand how to protect my space and feel more grounded about myself.

Throughout that year, my Mom had a friend from the youth named Jack who wrote a book. She was really interested in reading this book so she purchased it. It was called One Wish Won Battle. As she started to read this book she was blown away. It was all about his spiritual journey and how he started to see things. He went through some pretty amazing things that were like being in a completely different world. She was blown away and reached out to him through Facebook. She started discussing with him how I was going through similar things.

She took me out to lunch one day after reading his book. She said, "I really understand you now Annabelle. You have a gift like this too. This book opened my eyes to your reality." I told my Mom that day all about what I felt and could see. I went on with endless stories of my life. She insisted that I talked to her friend Jack over the phone once we got home from lunch.

Once we got home, we waited for his phone call. He was just getting off of work his time. I was a shy timid girl at the time, so talking to any stranger for me was a challenge. For a while our home didn't feel as peaceful as it should. My brother was also energy sensitive, but he couldn't see things like I could. He would feel the weird dark energy in the house or souls around, but he couldn't see. That made him afraid, so he started to sleep next to my parents' bed on the floor. We didn't know how to help at the time because we didn't know anyone who could help in that aspect.

The phone started ringing and my Mom immediately picked up. "Jack? It's so good to hear from you! This is truly amazing!" Jack and my Mom didn't speak until today. They hadn't talked to one another in over twenty-five years. They spoke for a few minutes about everything. My Mom eventually handed over the phone to me. I took the phone and spoke to him like he was my best friend. It was the easiest and most comfortable phone call I ever had with a stranger. I was not normally like this with strangers. I spoke with him about my clairvoyancy and he spoke to me about his. All the sudden, I saw many angels come into our home. I saw them clearing out the dark energies and destroying any Demons and Spirits. My Dad and brother at this time were at the store.

Jack spoke, "Do you see and feel anything around you in this moment?" I said, "Yes, I see a bunch of Angels clearing out the home of dark energies, Demons and Spirits." He laughed and said, "Yes, I sent out a legion of angels to your house to clear any bad things that shouldn't be there." I was amazed and shocked. My brother and Dad came home later that day from the store. As my brother walked in, he said, "What happened in here? I feel so different and peaceful." He had no idea we just spoke to Jack on the phone. It was one of the most powerful moments of God's hands coming in through Jack to heal our home. I was truly amazed.

Jack was based out in Chicago while we lived in Colorado. He was telling us how he actually held many mediation classes throughout the month on Saturdays. If you lived far away, it was no problem because he also had people attend the class over the phone. This meditation class was amazing because it was completely led by God. It was completely faith based. We decided as a family that we would like to all take the mediation class and learn how to let more of the Lord into our home.

On a Saturday in September of that year, we all got ready to take Jacks meditation class over the phone. We were all a little nervous because we didn't know what to expect. I didn't feel weird about this class at all compared to that other one I took. Jack was being led completely by God and that other lady was not. As we got ready to start, Jack told everyone that the angels from the Lord were protecting the class from any foreign negative energies. We were all safe to look inward and let go of our blockages we may or may not have.

He went on to explain the charkas and the purpose of the charkas. How the Lord created us from earth and cosmic energy and how we would use that in today's class. Throughout the class, we would go through each charka and ground ourselves to the center of the earth. We ground ourselves to the center of the earth to let go of any negative energy or blockages that get in our own way. The center of the earth burns up any negative energies because it is completely light and lava. Being in this class taught me that we get in our own ways. It's our job to look inward and let go of anything that is holding us back from being who we need to be for eternal life. We are all human, and we all have our issues. It's up to us whether we want to push past our own insecurities to change ourselves for the better and to grow our relationship with the Lord, Jesus and Holy Spirit.

As we continued through the class, it was the first time I realized how centered and peaceful I felt. We learned how to cope with our own space and how to protect our space. Our space is our own energy and life. The people around us are always in our hearts, but we don't want people to sit and stay in our own bubble. They could feed off of our energy and create anxiety without even knowing it. The Lord created meditation and having your own space for a reason. That reason is to reflect inward and understand yourself. You cannot change anyone but yourself. It's like raising children, therefore you are there to help them grow in themselves. Each and every one of us is made differently by God. Even if you are born and have family genetics; we are souls made and created by the Lord.

Throughout the class as we were going through the meditation in our charkas and space, Jack introduced us to our inner selves. It's the way we see ourselves and what is going on in our space. We call them spirit guides. They are created by the Lord and have no souls. They are good spirits that reflect who we are and what we may be dealing with internally. It is how you are able to see yourself in each charka and go through different things. Once you pass away, they get recycled into the earth and paired with someone else. They also could come back in the form of an animal or insect etc. This is the reason many people think they have had past lives because their spirit guide had one and not the person themselves. Our soul cannot be reborn, once we die, we go into eternity and wait until Jesus is ready to take us home.

After the class we thanked Jack for helping us tremendously. It changed our lives for the better. I no longer struggled with panic attacks as bad as they were or anxiety that was crippling.

This also helped my brother and parents as well. The one thing that has always stuck with me even to this day is, the Lord will never give you more than you can handle. Even if it seems like you can't handle it. The Lord always has his reasons for allowing you to go through the fire and flames in this life. Yet again, who would we be if we didn't go through anything?

Jack wanted to speak with our family after the class was completely over. Once everyone else had left the class on his end he spoke with us about the mediation class. He wanted to make sure we understood what was going on and how to help ourselves through meditating by ourselves when we needed to. I absolutely loved it and was grateful for the right help and biblical truth. He also wanted to talk to us alone because he wanted tell me something. He explained to me that he was in charge of this team of energy healers. The Lord put the team together to have the sole purpose be to protect the bride of Christ. At the time I didn't know what that truly meant, but the Lord wanted me to be a part of the team. In time, I was to find out that truly meant being there and taking care of all of mankind on earth and in eternity. It was a huge thing for a fifteen-year-old girl who was still finding her way in life.

Jack was unsure of the Lords plan for me to be on the team at the time because of how young I was. I completely understood that. I was immature and still finding myself in life. That was a huge responsibility for me. I was learning what clairvoyance meant to me and how to not trust everything I saw and protect my space. I had a hard time feeling what was the truth and what was not with my gut. I constantly needed training and help. Eventually, Jack wanted to come out to visit to train me in person for the team in helping others. The first thing he told me was, "You have to help yourself before you can help anyone else."

That winter Jack came out to Colorado for the first time in twenty-five years to train me for the team. I was excited and I know my parents were too. They hadn't seen Jack in twenty-five years and met each other through the day of the youth. My Dad and I went that night to go pick him up at the airport. Once we picked him up, it was like a family reunion of a relative we hadn't seen in years not just an old friend. We all stayed up that night until two in the morning just chatting in the kitchen talking about life and our spiritual journeys.

The next morning, we all got up and headed down stairs for some breakfast. We chatted and for days we were entranced by the amazing stories Jack had to tell us. I was so amazed by his stories; I could sit there day in and out just hearing about eternity. He talked about how angels are given to us for protection from the Lord once we are baptized. Normally, people have one angel with them that protects them from that moment on. In the New Apostolic church, we have baptism and holy sealing. The baptism is usually done by the Priest while the holy sealing is done by the Apostle. The baptism indicates that you are now a friend of God. You are a part of his circle in faith and it is done with water that is blessed through prayer. Holy sealing indicates that you are now a child of God. This is through the Apostle laying his hands on the head of souls. To become a child of God is an amazing opportunity. You have the ability to become the bride of Christ; to live in his home with many rooms in the kingdom of Heaven.

In this life, we strive to become more like Christ. This is our learning ground. We learn through the sins and mistakes we make so we can be better for eternal life and become who we need to be. Who God created us to be for eternal life which is our true selves. We all have amazing and unique personalities and gifts that God has made. We were made different for a reason and its beautiful. That is who we truly are in Gods image.

While Jack was visiting, he held a meditation class from my parent's house for that weekend. Some people came from the church and some of our family friends as well. Every time Jack held a meditation class, I felt like I would learn something new about myself or a new technique. When you first meditate, it may take time for your body to adjust. The body itself has a hard time sitting and focusing on the energy through meditation. When I first meditated my body was completely grumpy with me and was not use to it at all. You can also feel hot or tinging in places as you meditate or run energy through your body the first couple of times or many times. My mom had a hard time with meditation because she could not see or feel anything. It can be challenging to get adjusted to meditation but don't give up! It just takes practice.

After the class had left for the day, I started to see three angels standing around me. One stood beside me on my left-hand side and had short dark brown hair with brown eyes. He wore a white robe like Jesus but they had armor that was silver and gold. He had a huge sense of humor and liked to joke around but he also served and protected. The next angel that was on my right side was named Marticus. He was very strong with large muscles. He had long blonde hair and blue eyes. He also had a white robe as well as silver and gold armor. Also, he didn't have much of a sense of humor. He was more serious with not much emotion. The last angel stood behind me and his name was Articus. He had sense of humor but also was serious; it was a split down the middle personality. His hair was blonde and long and eyes were also blue.

Seeing all of this was so eye opening to me. The Lord protects us and keeps us safe from Satan's crap. He is always with us and bigger than any negative energy or thing we may be facing in this life. Even if we don't understand the Lords plan for our life or even the afterlife in eternity, there is always a reason for what he allows for us.

As we were all sitting together with my family and Jack, I started seeing more things in that moment. I started seeing two figures, one a woman and one a man. The woman had reddish brown hair and had blue eyes. Her hair was put up into a pony tail and she had everyday clothes on like jeans and a shirt. She was so jumpy and bouncy just filled with bubbly energy of excitement. The man next to her was bald and very timid and quiet. He also had blue eyes and everyday clothing like jeans and a shirt. He was very logic and concentrated ready to tackle anything with a calm manner. I was so confused and said, "Jack, I see these people here by me. Who are they?" He said, "Ask them their names." I looked to them and asked them who they were. The lady was so excited she looked as if she was going to pee her pants. The man was embarrassed and shook his head saying, "Will you calm down Andrea?" She giggled and said, "I'm trying Matt; I'm trying!" She was running in circles trying to calm herself down. Jack spoke and said, "They were supposed to wait until I introduced them to you, but they couldn't wait."

As I sat there, I wondered who these people were. They showed up and Jack knew who they were. I was seriously confused. "I know your probably confused here, but these people are your healing masters. They will help you when you give others energy healings in the future. God created them from your energy and they have been waiting for this moment for centuries to meet you." Andrea was made up of my personality when I get very loving and bubbly. Like a light that bounces off a million energy balls. Matt was more of my logical and serious side. It is more quiet, timid and concentrated. I was completely blown away. These people that stood before me were not spirits, they were me. Just like when there are the Lord, Jesus and Holy Spirit, it is all God in one, but they are also separate energy beings.

I felt as if I were in a dream. I couldn't believe what was happening, it was just amazing more than words could describe. "The Lord has also given you a name Olivia. Everyone on the team has a name the Lord has given them other than their actual name. He calls you Radiance." Everyone on the team had some pretty amazing names like Firelight and Starlight. Jacks name was Supplanter. People on the team were also given a number that reflected an apostle in the bible. It was who we reflected as people. Mine was Apostle Thomas. I was amazed that my personality to the Lord was like Apostle Thomas and that I was created this way by the Lord. I was by no means an Apostle, but I was called to help protect the bride of Christ and help people in any way I could.

After the class and talking for a while with all the unbelievable things that were happening, Jack wanted to give me a healing to show me what it was like. He wanted to train me on how to properly give a faith-based healing. We went outside to sit on the deck in a chair because the weather was so nice that day. As he began to start the energy healing, we prayed and welcomed the Lord to have Jack be the vessel for the healing for any kind of help I needed for not only my charkas, but my physical body too. Everything was in the Lords hands.

It was an interesting healing because my dog Missy came outside to be around us at the time. She went over to the fence in the corner and just stood there the whole time staring us down. She didn't move or anything. All she did was tilt her head from side to side in confusion. For that whole hour of the energy healing, I laughed hysterically. I had a hard time keeping a straight face when I had never ever seen my dog act that way before. It was hilarious! Even though I was mostly laughing uncontrollably, the healing was amazing. Every chakra we got to Jack could see and feel everything I was going through inertially. It was like reading a book and figuring out what parts of life I needed to let go of and heal from. Then we saw what places were flourishing and I didn't need much help in those areas. Once he got to the last part of the healing, he placed his hands on my head. One hand on my forehead and the other on the back of my head. He said, "I heal you in Jesus name." As he said those words I felt and saw a rush of the light blue healing energy run through my entire body and chakras. It destroyed any evil or negative energy in my space and helped heal my physical body.

Everything is in God's hands when you have a healing. It's not a miracle like Jesus did when he was on earth. This practice is just being a vessel for the Lord and running cosmic and earth energy through the person that may need help or guidance. The spiritual energy healers (like Andrea and Matt) the Lord gave allows the vessel to be able to help that person in clearing things that may be blocking their space. They go into the charkas and cut down the barriers that block a person from healing or moving forward in life.

You never ever want to just give someone an energy healing if you are not called to do so, or if you do not know how to properly give one. It's very serious and involves another life. You never want to put yourself or anyone else in harm's way just because you want to give it a shot. The Lord called Jack and the team to be able to handle this the correct and safe way. Just like teaching a faith-based meditation class. If you do not protect the space of the class or have any guidelines from the Lord on how to do so, you should not teach this and put yourself or others in harm's way.

Chapter 5

As time went on and I was figuring out my clairvoyancy, I was also trying to get to know my helpers Andrea and Matt. I was practicing on what Jack had taught us in meditation class. I had a hard time meditating some days; for some reason it was challenging for me to ground myself and what not. Andrea and Matt would connect into my hands to help with various things like grounding and running energy through my body if I was having a rough time. I could send them to family and friends to help ground them as well or if they were experiencing anything troubling.

I went through a night of an extreme head ache because my body was trying to physically adjust to the pure energy that Andrea and Matt carried. They were not people with souls, just pure energy created from the Lord so they had no sin. They were just made up of my energy from the Lord. It's almost like genetics when you have a child, but it's an exact replica of yourself. It's also similar to when they say you can't see the face of God or you die. The energy of the Lord is so powerful it's too great for us humans in our sinful nature and body.

After sometime being around other people for tutoring or teaching Violin lessons, there were people who would stand around me for too long and feel the need to run to the bathroom. This would happen because I was in training for the team and I carried a great amount of pure energy from Andrea and Matt. My body just got used to it over time so I didn't really realize the effect it had on others. It truly flushed out there system not only physically, but energy wise too for the better.

One day as I was relaxing around the house, I decided that it was time to get some sun shine outside. I went to go sit on the trampoline we had in the backyard. At one point we had a jungle gym with a swing, but as we got older my parents traded it for a trampoline. As I was approaching the trampoline, I saw two figures of men standing in front of me. One had reddish brown hair that was long as well as a beard. His eyes were blue and green and had the appearance of biblical robes that they wore back in that time period. He was wearing a white robe with a rope around his waist for a belt. Also, he had sandals. The other man was behind him and he was timid. Brown and short hair is what this man had as well as brown eyes. He was wearing the same thing the other man wore.

I went up to them puzzled and said, "Who are you guys?" The long haired one laughed and said, "My name is Apostle Peter and behind me is Apostle James." James waved at me and smiled, then he timidly went back behind Peter. I laughed and said, "Wow, this is amazing! I can't believe this! God bless you both!" I was in complete shock. James stepped out again and said, "We are here to give you a cloche of peace." They threw this green color over me that looked like a see-through blanket. This was going to help me through the challenges I would face ahead.

We walked into the house together and I got to the dining room table. As I sat down, they sat down next to me. Peter on one side and James on the other. Suddenly, Jesus appeared before us and said, "Hey guys, it's like old times. Remember the last supper?" We all laughed. Jesus took a seat across from me and we all sat together for a few minutes. My mom was in the kitchen for the moment and I called her over to tell her what was happening. She was blown away and shocked. Peter, James, Jesus and I all sat together for a while just chatting away and laughing together. After a while they had to go, but I was thankful and humbled to have had those moments with them.

Later that day I decided to go for a drive and take my dog Missy to McDonalds. She loved riding with me in the car to get her favorite vanilla ice cream cone. She was so smart she knew what a lot of things meant. On our way to get the ice cream, I felt two people from eternity in the back seat. One man had the staff of Moses and was wearing a pure white robe. He had a long beard and longer hair that was white. The other man was wearing a colorful robe and he had a golden crown on his head. His hair was also long with a long beard, but he had dark black hair. I looked behind me when we parked in the parking lot of McDonalds and said, "Who are you guys?" They smiled at me and the white-haired guy said, "I'm Moses and this is David. We wanted to hang out with you and meet you today." I was shocked and said, "Why me? I'm just a regular person. You both are amazing! I can't believe you are here!" They smiled and gave me cloches of peace, strength, and love. I kept seeing and feeling so many things from eternity it was truly like a dream to me.

As the months went on after January of my 10th grade year, I had a few moments to myself after my online classes ended. I was taking all of my work online at the time. It was easier for me because I delt with a lot of anxiety at the time. I was still learning on how to ground myself and meditate so everything took time.

I went into my parents' room where my dog Missy was laying on the bed. She loved to sun bathe in my parents' bed all spaced out. She was definitely a sun dog. The winter was hard on her because she didn't have much fur. She would run outside to go to the bathroom and run straight back into the house. In the summer, she would bask in the beams of sunlight and try to chase the squirrels on the fence. As feisty as she was, she loved her family.

As I came to sit next to her and snuggle, I suddenly got a vision from the Lord. I found myself sitting on a cloud and in front of me was Jesus, Father, and Holy Spirit. I turned to look behind me and saw many souls; there were more than I could count. I felt like I was in front of legions and legions of people and angels from all time periods throughout history. I looked to Father, Jesus and Holy Spirit in complete disbelief. I started to cry from the immense love and light I could feel not only from Father, Jesus and Holy Spirit, but from eternity as well. There were many people from different walks of faith or paths. Many ages of all kinds we standing behind me looking to Father.

The Lord spoke and said, "Today, I ask you Radiance a big question as you stand here before me. Will you serve my people of all eternity and all of earth?" I stood there in complete shock. The Lord was giving me an opportunity to not only serve his people of earth, but also eternity. To protect the bride of Christ. I fell to my knees crying saying, "Why me? I am not greater than anyone on this earth or eternity. I am nearly a sinful human. I don't deserve anything." The Lord spoke, "I chose you Olivia, to do my work. To be a vessel for my work. Just like the Apostles, I have chosen to do my work as vessels for me and my people."

As I bowed my head on my knees, Jesus came over in front of me. He stated, "Olivia, do you accept to be a vessel of the Lords work? To help and protect the bride of Christ for all living and departed souls?" I cried and replied, "Yes, I do." As he stood over me, he had a staff that looked like the staff of Moses. He put the staff to one shoulder and then the next. As he did this, I saw light blue energy of healing and protection go into me. This would help when I would give any energy healings to heal or clear out any negative energy in someone's space. I cried for a good thirty minutes or so during this and after. It was one of the most powerful experiences of my life.

I got up from my parents' room and ran to my mom to tell her what had just happened. She was completely blown away as well. I went ahead to text Jack because I was completely blown away by what had happened. He responded and was surprised as well. Jack had no idea this was supposed to happen. Only me and someone else on the team had the blue energy for the moment. There was a total of nine people on the team so far at that time. The Lord was planning on having a total of twelve of us like the twelve Apostles. Eventually in time, the team was to grow to seventy-two people. It is a huge job and honor to help and protect the bride of Christ.

From that point on, I had many different encounters; especially on Halloween. Halloween use to be a day of prayer and support for eternity. To honor those who have passed before us. Now it is Satan's playground. The day is full of scary dead skeletons and all about fear. Dressing up for fun is one thing, but being scary and full of blood and guts is not what it should be about. People don't realize that when you allow scary things like this or movies even into the home, you are allowing dark spirits and demons into your home. There are even demons that get attached to objects like skeletons and scary things. I've walked by homes with all that crap outside and I see them. I've had them growl at me and try to attack me like a bad guard dog. Be careful what you allow into your home. For your own sake and your families.

In eternity when one passes away, they go to what we call Realms or they walk the earth by where they passed away. Realms are like the holding space where people wait until the return of Christ to come. There is a Realm called the Paradise. It's exactly how it sounds which is full of light and all good things of the Lord, Jesus and Holy Spirit. What you do in that realm can be many things, including helping those who are in darker realms. For an example, when my grandpa on my mom's side pasted away, I could see him. We had a very good relationship together and were very close. He knew I could see him so he would play tricks with me. He would move objects and turn on sinks. He would giggle and jump around like a child in faith. He would come to me many times to encourage me or encourage the family. In the realms, he was in the realm of paradise, so he would go down into the darker realms for a few days to help people who were suffering or being tormented by demons. When he would do this, he would also go with a man we knew growing up in the church Joe. Joe was an amazing man of faith as well and passed around a similar time as my grandpa did. They worked side by side in the realms doing the work of the Lord and probably still do to this day.

The other realms that are in eternity are unknown, but some of them are known. The darkest realm you can go to in eternity is called the unredeemed. These are the souls that have had trouble on earth with murdering others or not having forgiveness in their hearts. It is a very dark and horrible place. People who are stuck in this realm have to go through horrific things. One example is of this realm is if you were put to death on the cross by the demons who control the dark realm or anyone else who has evil in that realm, you would die and go through it all over again because your soul can not pass away. Your soul is not like your body; it is purely energy. Even some people who are stuck in that realm get their limbs pulled apart and go through horrendous things over and over again. Eternity has no time so there is no break. The only help these souls get is by others that have come from a higher realm that reach out and invite them to service for the departed at church. I cannot imagine the terrible things that must go on for them. It's like hell itself.

The last realm that I know of is addiction. If someone was addicted to smoking cigarettes, alcohol, or anything else, they would be sitting right in front of that addiction that they had on earth, but they wouldn't be able to reach it. They would crave it worse than ever before and sit completely stuck feeling that way twenty-four seven.

Once when my mom, grandma and I all went out to eat after church one Sunday, I could feel the presence of my grandpa. He was very close to my grandma a lot and would watch over her while he was in eternity. We all sat at our favorite Mexican place called Las Delicious. They had amazing Mexican food for really good prices and they were always very quick with the food. We talked together for a while and my grandpa was just chilling out next to me and grandma. I was telling them how he was with us and loved and missed us so much. While I was telling them, I suddenly felt many souls standing behind me. I quickly turned around and saw many departed souls behind my grandpa. Many of them had chains on their hands with the darkness of their sins. They were weighed down by the weight of their sin and looked directly at me. The emotions I felt at the time were just pure humility and grief.

My grandpa stood closer to me and took one knee to the floor. He put his hands in my lap and he looked up to me and said, "Olivia, will you pray for these people?" Service for the departed was the following Sunday and I could feel all of the urgency to help and pray. As I started to pray for the line of souls, I saw the angels from the Lord appear and stand by the souls. After I prayed, I saw the angels take the souls where they needed to be for the upcoming service for the departed. My grandpa stood up and smiled and said, "Thanks." I nodded my head and started to cry. The experience was truly humbling because we are all sinners. We all need one another that is how the Lord created us. Just like the human body needs many things and organs to function; it's the same with our reality. We are not made to do life alone.

Going back to my high school years in eleventh grade to be exact, I was still learning on how to manage feeling and seeing things. There were times when would see things and it wasn't really Jesus or positive things like Angels. The experiences that I have talked about have been real, but there have been times where demons would disguise themselves and pretend to be people or positive beings like Jesus or Angels. Over time, I had to learn to trust my gut. Everything your gut feels about people or things is always right. For example, when you are supposed to go somewhere or do something, but your gut feeling is having a bad feeling about something or someone; always listen to that. I wasn't listening to my gut when I was younger and I fell for these kinds of evil shenanigans. Please don't do what I did and always listen to your gut instinct first. Sometimes our emotions can easily take over things and we can easily get sucked into anything. You don't want to listen to your heart, you always listen to your gut.

In the fall of my eleventh-grade year, my family and I decided to go out to eat one afternoon after church service. We were all mourning that day because we recently heard the news that my cousin Mark passed away suddenly. He was only nineteen at the time of his passing and so many of us were still in shock. My heart was heavy with sadness and grief. I could also feel everyone else's mourning too. It was an over load of emotions that I could not express in words. Mark was an amazing person. He was always kind to everyone and had many good friends. Mark was a Christian at one point in time during his childhood when he was younger, but as he got older, he turned to atheism.

He was driving home from being a DJ for a club one night in a city called Castle Rock. Colorado has many hills and mountains which makes driving a little more hazardous; especially in snow or rainy weather. It was snowing that night and there were a lot of curves going around the mountain. He was going extremely fast around the corners to the point of where he slid off the corner and off of the cliff that was there. He went down hundreds of feet into the valley of the mountain. The car itself flipped over multiple times and he was instantly crushed without the seat belt on.

We all ate some awesome Mexican food at the three Margaritas and just chatted about everything going on. All of the sudden, I felt a presence near me and I knew right away it was Mark. Mark was in total shock that he was now on the other side in eternity. He could read everyone's thoughts and see everyone's emotions. When one passes away, you truly see everything someone may be dealing with. Everything that was on the inside is now on the outside when you pass. He was scared because he didn't know what to do. He saw that I could see him so he hung around me like glue to my side. After being an atheist, he saw that God was certainly real and that it was no joke to being in eternity on the other side. I texted Jack and told him that Mark was scared and he didn't know what to do. Jack responded and said, "Pray for the angels to take him where he needs to go."

The angels came once we were finished with our food and on our way back to the car. My dad was actually starting to see and feel things more after he took Jacks meditation class. The Lord was allowing him to have insight as to what I could see and feel. My dad turned around and said, "Mark is sitting in the back seat now. There is an angel of white light sitting next to him on his left side and a dark one sitting next to him on his right side." I texted Jack back to let him know what was happening with Mark. He responded and said, "Pray for Mark. He unfortunately had to go with the dark angel because he chose to believe in atheism." From that day on I prayed for Mark every chance I could to remember him.

A couple months later, we had our regular Wednesday night service for the month. We switched from every Wednesday night to just one night a month on Wednesdays. I was sitting in the church pews just listening to the service when I felt and saw Mark out of nowhere. He was helping someone and lifting them off of the ground. The persons energy was so weak that they didn't have the strength from their own sins to carry forward. Mark was helping them and pulling them up to the angels so they could help the soul and take the soul where it needed to be in eternity. He turned around and smiled at me and said, "Thank you for praying for me. I'm in a much better place now. I help people." I couldn't help but cry and smile back. The Lord is amazing he truly is. We can help so many people living or departed just through the power of prayer. Also, seeing what others may go through here or in eternity helps us understand Gods plan for us all better. God wants all of us to be with him in eternity and it is up to us whether we accept that offer to humble ourselves and help in the Lords work. To me Mark is not a cousin, he is a brother. Our relationship on earth was not very close, but in eternity we became very close.

Chapter 6

John 14:6 "I am the way, the truth and the life." This is the bible verse I love to go to because the Lord, Jesus and Holy Spirit are our whole lives. They are pure and loving light; like a candle that burns a flame without a shadow and having no darkness. We may not have all of the answers, but walk by faith not sight. I've had my own moments of doubt and human sin. The Lord has always helped me through my own blindness and sinful nature. It's especially true now a days as we reach the end time. There are four angels that hold the four corners of the earth with vales of peace, love, light and etc. Once they are commanded by the Lord to let go, all chaos will break through. It will be Satan's playground of hell on earth while Jesus comes to take those of whom he chooses with him to the bride's feast in Heaven. He will come to take those in eternity first and those who are on earth second. Good will become evil to many and evil become good. The truth will always be biblical. It is not about religion and rules. It is truly about relationship and where your heart is; the character you have and what you have gone through. Growing into who the Lord created you to be for eternal life and having that relationship with them.

As I was growing in my clairvoyancy, I was still struggling to find myself and get a handle with being on the team. I was almost past my teenage years to my twenties, but still immature. I had some growing and maturity to face to be able to really understand the team and what that truly meant. As I was trained more and more over the period of some years and I learned how to give someone a proper energy healing.

One of my mom's friends at the time from her bible study group was struggling with some health issues. She was emotionally and mentally drained from the toll her body was taking on her. Hospital after hospital she was really struggling with everything. My mom referred her to have a possible energy healing and told her I could possibly help her. She came over one day for the healing to take place; I could feel the pain she was carrying with her not only physically but also emotionally.

Before we began, I prayed with her to the Lord and asked him to be in this session. For me to be the vessel for whatever his will for this lady was. Suddenly I felt the Lord come very close to both of us and the angels guard around us. I had Andrea and Matt start the cleansing process. As I stood there, I started to see everything that was blocked in her system and causing her physical pain. Sometimes when our charkas become blocked, we can get different kinds of physical things. It just depends on the person because everyone is different. If you think about it this way, it's like adding on negative stress or more water to a cup that is already full. If the cup over fills, it has no place to go. Just like our body if we hold onto things or have too much stress it will cause problems and blockages. This is why meditation just like exercise is so important. We need to let go to empty that cup and fill it back up with healing and positive energy.

As I went through each charka and pushed the cosmic energy and earth energy through, Andrea and Matt were working hard to tackle the blockages to get it out of her space. Sometimes, we can even have negative spirits and demons that may lurk in our spaces and try to stick around. That can really throw us off and make us feel like something is really up. Satan's crap likes to drag us humans down in any way they can through playing on our own fear and sin. We can pray for them to leave our spaces and have angels destroy them, but sometimes they just don't like to leave that easy. This lady didn't have anything in her space, but I have had others that have had things. When those moments come, I would text Jack and have him come in and destroy it with some of the other angels. Jack had the authority from the Lord to be able to do this and travel spiritually. His soul never leaves his body, just his spirit guide.

Once all of the negative things were destroyed and pulled out, we replenished her with her own energy through a golden bubble of light that goes right above their head. You call the energy back from all of the places you have been to and watch it fill up like a balloon. Once it is full, you can add things to this like light, love, healing, peace, and much more positive things from the Lord. This golden energy that is your energy is put back into the body by popping the golden bubble. It runs down like honey if you poured it on your head. It goes into your space and body and reaches you to a cellular level. After this, I placed my hands on her head and said, "I heal you in the name of Jesus." I saw the blue energy of healing and protection run out of my hands and into her body from the Lord.

After the healing had ended, I told her to drink plenty of fluids because flushing out the system like this is just like getting a deep tissue massage. The only difference is you are clearing out all the toxic negative energy in the space that is no longer needed. It helps the body itself heal at a cellular and physical level. Everything in an energy healing is in the Lords hands. The healing comes from him and we are just vessels here to help in his work and his plan. I also informed her that she should be putting up her rose flowers around her space for protection.

I did many other healings from that day forward for a while. I felt very honored to be able to help in the Lords work and help his people. It was very humbling for me. As I continued on, I was still having trouble listening to my gut and finding my place on the team. I was so young and I didn't know myself very well yet. I was still immature and figuring out my way. Jack knew I was struggling so he suggested a visit out to the other team members out in Michigan. I was really excited to meet the other team members. I felt like I was bugging Jack a lot with all my questions and just getting overly excited to finally talk to someone who understood what I was seeing.

That summer after graduation of senior year, I flew out for the first time in my life completely alone to stay with complete strangers on the team that I had never met in person before. I would text or phone call getting to know them and at times also asking them for advice. I was nervous, but also excited. It was a big milestone for me to travel without family.

That morning, my mom dropped me off at the airport. I got out of the car and gave her a big hug goodbye. It was an exciting next journey for me to grow more within myself. The lines inside the airport were very long and it was a long wait to get to my gate. After I got through the line, I went to the under-ground train that Denver had to get to all of the gates. The Denver airport was huge so everything took a tremendous amount of time. Once I got to my gate, I decided to grab a quick coffee and some snacks for the long air plane ride ahead. They opened the doors to aboard the plane and I got into my seat near the window. Airplanes always made me feel weird and anxious because it was so many people stuck together in such a small space. It almost felt like you could sit on the persons lap that was sitting next to you. I was on my first plane ride of two. The first ride went to the Chicago Illinois airport. Once I got there, I would transfer to the plane that went straight to Kalamazoo Michigan.

The plane ride over to Chicago went fairly smoothly. Once we took off the ground, I could see the Lords hand hold up the plane and all of the angels just flying right beside the plane.

It comforted me and made me feel safe. When we landed in Chicago, I texted Jack to see if he could feel my energy as I landed in his state. He responded saying, "Yes! Just as you crossed over into the state from the plane, I knew you were here." It was truly amazing how sensitive we all were to each other and energy on the team.

As I walked through the Chicago airport, I noticed how different the energy was there from Colorado. It wasn't as laid back and much more city like. They loved their hotdogs and had many different options for the hotdog. I was completely blown away by the different culture. It was truly amazing! I was trying to find my gate for Kalamazoo Michigan before it was too late. I didn't want to miss my flight, but Chicago's airport was so much bigger than Denver's was. I thought Denver's airport was big, but it was nothing in comparison to Chicago. Once I arrived to the gate for Kalamazoo, I texted Linda and Skylar the two other healers that were on the team. I was going to stay with Linda and her family first and then Skylar's second. Linda was about eight or so years older than me with three kiddos of her own. Her kids were all a little younger than I was. Skylar was about twenty or so years older than me one child that was older than I was.

Finally boarding the last plane, I took my seat next to another window seat. This plane was much smaller than the one from Denver to Chicago and only had about twenty passengers. It was very empty, but I liked that because I liked having my space. When the plane took off, we traveled completely over the whole lake of Michigan. There was no land in sight the whole entire plane ride over to Kalamazoo. It was also a lot shorter of a plane ride than Denver to Chicago. It was more tolerable for me. Once we landed. I got off the plane and went to go find my luggage. It took a little while to wait for the luggage, but finding my way around was a lot easier. It was a tiny airport compared to the other two I was at that day.

Walking to the lower level, I could see Linda and Skylar waiting there for me. I waved from the escalator as I was coming down. I finally made it down and we all greeted each other with hugs. It was so nice to finally meet them in person. I was over the moon with excitement. As we walked over to Skylar's car, we were all talking about the team and how excited we all were for the week and weekend ahead. Jack was going to drive out later that Friday evening after he got off of work to Kalamazoo. He only lived about three hours away at the time so it was an easier travel and drive. I was going to stay at Linda's house first for the first couple of days and then Skylar's.

Once we got to Linda's house we were greeted by her dogs. She had two bigger dogs that were so gentle and kind. Her house was filled with so much love and light especially for her family. It was a nice cosey little house. We sat at the kitchen table for a long time just chatting about life and sharing our stories. It was so nice to talk to people who had the same kind of perspective as I did. Its hard living life feeling alone in seeing and feeling things.

After some time had passed Linda had to go pick up the kiddos from school and so did Skylar. I left the house with Linda and we said our goodbyes to Skylar. Jack had another Saturday meditation class the following couple days at Linda's in laws house. Jack was going to stay the night at Linda's in laws house so he could teach the class in the morning and then go to church with us on Sunday morning. We picked up Linda's kids from the school and I got to know them a little more as well. I stayed in Linda's daughter room while I was there and her daughter stayed in the two boys' rooms. The two boys slept on the couch. Her family was so real with one another and so close. I wasn't judged and I was loved for who I was and where I was at. It was refreshing that we could all have different perspectives about things and still have the same love in our hearts for one another.

That night as I was getting ready for bed, I prayed to the Lord telling him how thankful I was to be a vessel and apart of his work in this experience. That weekend I was there was also Pentecost so we were all preparing ourselves for that service as well. The next morning, we all woke up pretty early so Linda could take the kids to school. I wasn't use to how early everyone woke up because I was two hours behind Michigan time. Getting up at 6am their time was like getting up at 4am my time in Denver.

Driving back to Linda's house after dropping the kids off at school was awesome. Michigan was so much more humid than Colorado was. It was easier for me to breathe having the air be more humid and also not being a mile high. There was more oxygen and more trees. It was like a forest that was full of nutrients and lots of greenery. It was very cloudy that morning and not too sunny. It had much more cloudy days than sunny. I remember my grandma telling me stories about Michigan and how they had one point where it was cloudy for two weeks at one point.

Getting back to the house, Linda and I sat at the kitchen table once again just chatting away about our spiritual journeys. We talked about the team and how crazy everything has been. We each had our own different gifts when it came to seeing and feeling things. We all had our own journey, but it was amazing to be understood. I learned from Linda from her experiences and what she had to go through. We have all had to go through our own tests of faith in one way or another to grow and to learn. One of the things I learned from being out there was grounding. I learned that some people without knowing can ground to you instead of the center of the earth. Its more common with family members or children and mothers. This happens when the person who is grounding to the other tries to control the other in all kinds of different aspects. It can make the person who is being grounded to very anxious or feel somewhat sick. We were made to have our own space and ground to the center of the earth and not one another. It can cause some serious problems in relationships and people being too controlling. The Lord made us all individuals and we need to be respectful of all spaces. We are all our own people and we have our own lives. Being controlled will not be helpful to anyone, but only hinder relationships. The key to having a successful and healthy relationship is having boundaries and support. Unconditional love is the answer.

As the day went on, it was time to pick the kids up from school. We went to the school and picked them up and then went back to the house. Before it became evening, one of Linda's brothers Sam stopped by to get an energy healing from me. You can give energy healings to family, but it is harder because they are family. It's a little easier to give a stranger or friend a healing. It was really nice outside that evening as the sun was going down so we decided to do the healing outside.

As I began the energy healing, I did what I normally did. I prayed for the Lord to be the center and for me to be the vessel. The angels stood to protect the space and I started running the cosmic and earth energy through. Something was off while I was giving that healing. It didn't feel the same as the other healings I had given. Andrea and Matt felt very distant in my space and not the same. Linda stepped in during the healing to help me because she felt like something was completely off as well. It wasn't right. We weren't sure what was going on so we decided to wait until Jacks meditation class for the next morning to see if he knew what was going on.

We had a big campfire in the backyard with all of her family later that night. It was so nice just sitting with everyone and talking about anything and everything. I was accepted. It was like going from close minded to very open minded about everything. Life wasn't just about what kind of work you did or college you went to, it was about the kind of person you were to everyone else. Who you are in your heart? You can chase your dreams, but ultimately, our goal is to be like Jesus. To be our true selves who the Lord created us to be. The one thing I have always admired about Linda is that she would give it to me straight. She would never sugar coat anything and she would always tell me the truth even if it hurt. It was like taking a big piece of humble pie. I didn't need good manners or punctuality to be accepted.

That night as we all went to bed, I started feeling really off. I felt anxious out of nowhere on and off and weird sensations of darkness around me. Everyone was asleep and I didn't want to wake anyone up so I tried to ground myself and meditate and clear out my space. Nothing seemed to be helping and my body started getting physically ill. I took deep breaths in and out slowly thinking I might be getting sick with the stomach flu or something. I wasn't getting a fever or anything, but it was throwing me for a loop. I grabbed my plastic grocery sack I kept in my bag just in case as I was about ready to hurl, only I couldn't hurl. It was the worst feeling ever.

As I finally fell asleep in the early morning, I felt like something was trying to attack me in my sleep. I woke up and went into the kitchen telling Linda what had happened in the night and into the early morning. She immediately texted Jack and told him as well. He verified that I was attacked in the night by a demon while everyone was asleep. He cleared my space and made sure it was gone once we all got to Linda's in laws house. They had many chairs for all of the people they had invited for this class. It was great because we had Linda, Skylar, Kaitlyn and Jacks brother Jordan all with us which was half of the healing team. There was a lot of amazing energy in the room for this meditation class. Each meditation class that Jacks held was always different. It had the same basics you would use for your own meditation, but it also had different moments. I always learned something new about myself.

Chapter 7
(Pentecost)

O nce the meditation class ended, I felt like I was frustrated or a little on edge. I wanted to know why the healing I gave Linda's brother went so funky and what had happened with Andrea and Matt. I felt stripped away and irritated. We all got food that Linda's in laws put together after that class and we sat down listening to Jacks stories. You could honestly sit there forever and hear his stories for hours. It is just amazing like a book of the bible, but not of the past just all in the present time.

We all went back and forth to be outside and then inside. It was a nice sunny day so all the kids played in the huge swimming pool they had in the backyard. It was so fun getting to know everyone on the team and getting to know all the people that attended the meditation class. It was the most relaxed atmosphere I had ever been at before. We would all joke around and relax with one another. It was hard for me at times because I was still trying to find myself. I didn't really love myself at the time and had a hard time maturing.

Once the later afternoon had hit, Jack wanted to take us all to Skylar's office she had for healings. We were going to have a meeting with all of the healers at that time. All of the other healers that were not with us physically had to call in for Jacks conference call. As we drove to the office, Jack was driving all crazy fast for fun. We turned sharp corners fast and the vehicle fled from one side to the other. We all laughed because we could see the angels that were protecting us all around the van holding it up from side to side as we turned. We were like, "Geeze Jack slow it down!"

The parking lot was empty as we approached the building. Everyone was off work because it was Saturday. Usually, they would come in and work Monday-Friday. As we went up the stairs and into her office, I could feel the good intensity of having everyone together. We all sat in a circle and got the other two healers on the line that could not be with us in person. Jack prayed over the team and as he prayed, we all held hands together. I could feel the most intense love and light I have ever felt in my life. We all started to ball our eyes out including Jack. We all lost our crap and just melted from the Lord's light and healing energy. We could all feel the love the Lord had for us all and the love we had for one another. I was so blown away. It felt like the time when the holy spirit descended for Pentecost. It was like a light of fire coming down.

We all finished the prayer and calmed down the energy in the room. It was a good intense energy of loving light and healing. It was pure and amazing. We all hugged and descended back down the stairs to the car. Jack was hilarious because when Kaitlyn got down by the car, he self-started the car from the hallway in the stairwell. She jumped up and said, "What the heck? Did I just do this?" We all laughed and Jack came out showing us the key fob and how he could self-start the car from where he was at. We truly treated each other like brothers and sisters we were so comfortable with one another.

Once we got back to the house, most of the people that attended the meditation class had left and gone back home. It was just a few other people now and the healers. I was still feeling off and on edge from giving Linda's brother that healing the other night before. Jack pulled me aside with Linda and Skylar to go inside while everyone else was outside. I sat across from them as they sat in front of me. I started to talk saying, "I don't understand what is going on in my space right now. I can't feel my team very well Andrea and Matt." Jack shrugged his head down and said, "Father informed me that he has taken your healing masters away from you at this time. Your maturity and manner in yourself has hindered you. You keep allowing to feel the wrong things in your space. You need to focus on yourself and be off of the team for now. Help yourself before you help others."

At that point in time was my time to grow in humility. It was like being punched in the gut, but honestly, I needed this. If I was not mature enough to be on the team and help others in this manner, I needed to be off of the team. At the time I was upset at the time and I didn't clearly see the bigger picture. By Father doing this, it allowed me to grow up and take responsibility for myself. I had to learn to love myself and forgive myself with my own sins.

Sitting there in tears, Jack spoke, "I'm so sorry Olivia. You also have a demon in your space that you have had ever sense you were a child. It has stayed hidden and fed off of your ego." Ego was a huge struggle for me which was hard for me to admit. At least I knew the truth and what needed to be mended from that point on. Sometimes in one way or another we all need to have our humble pie. It's what grows us in our character to who we become for eternal life. If we didn't go through anything in life, who would we be?

"I'm going to have Skylar give you a healing at her office. Linda will come with her." As Jack got up with us, I followed Skylar to her car and Linda came as well. We sat together as I cried in the car just trying to mend myself. Jack stayed behind at the house with everyone else. No one but us three knew what just happened. Driving along to the office a song started to play on the radio. It was a new song by Mercy Me called The Hurt and The Healer. The Lord always knew what kind of songs to play in the right moment and the right time. It was amazing to me because I was the hurt and Skylar was the healer.

When we entered the building again and walked up the stairs, we came to the main room once and I sat in the chair. This was the first time Skylar ever destroyed a demon in someone's space. Jack had the authority from Father, but once Father knew others would be ready, he allowed them that authority as well. We started the healing after we all got comfortable and took some deep breaths. Skylar started the healing and saw the demon in my space that was attached to me. She held out her hands as blue energy shot out of her hands and destroyed the demon. The whole time she was doing this she said that she felt like her hands were on fire from how powerful it was. Her name Father gave her was Firelight. Linda's name from Father was Starlight. Once that demon was destroyed, I felt like a part of myself just died because it was in my space for so long. I lived with that thing in my space most of my life. The ego just became normal to me. It was refreshing to have that thing gone though. I felt like a whole new person and felt more humility that I needed to be.

We hugged one another after the healing and I thanked Skylar for helping me. It was truly a huge awakening for me and humbling moment in my life. I wasn't easy, but it was worth it. We headed back down the stairs and into her car. She dropped Linda off at her in laws home while I went over to Skylar's house now to spend my second to last night I had in Michigan. I was touched when I stayed with Skylar. Her daughter had a friend who was homeless and living out of his car stay the night at their house for one night and use their shower like it was his own home. I appreciated all of the kindness and hospitality that Skylar and Linda showed me. They both didn't have much physically, but they were truly blessed by the people they had in their lives. Things don't matter, people do.

The next morning on Sunday we all woke up and got ready for Pentecost service. Even though I wasn't on the team itself anymore, I was still a part of the people who were on the team. I had a lot to work on within myself to mature and grow. Some people can't handle being on the team at any age. It's a lot of work and it is a lot of responsibility. Jack, Jordan, Linda, Skylar, Kaitlyn and I attended church that Sunday morning and after we all took a big group picture at the altar by the cross. Many church members looked over to us confused because we weren't related or anything. They didn't know anything about the team or the Lord's plan for his people yet. All in the Lords time is when everyone would know.

Later on, that day after church, Linda, Skylar and I went to the mall to walk around and look at things for a bit. I stopped in front of the glass and said, "I had the weirdest dream last night." They stopped and asked me what it was about. I went on to explain that I was a mermaid in the ocean. I got injured and I came to the shore. I got legs magically out of nowhere, but I was still injured. A man came to me and carried me on the land. He helped me learn how to walk on the land and treat my injury. Linda and Skylar both looked at one another and said, "This dream represents Jack taking you in and helping you on the team and with your gifts. Growing more in yourself."

All of my emotions were on a high because of everything I had gone through that weekend in Michigan. Going home was hard for me because I was leaving people who understood me and accepted me for who I was. I didn't conform to anyone and I was really stubborn in that way. I've always been different. When I got home, I told my parents all about my journey and what happened with the team. They were supportive and loved hearing about what happened. The bible verse that truly resonated with me during this time was James 3:17, "But the wisdom that comes from Heaven is first of all pure, then peace-loving, considerate, submissive, full of mercy and good fruit, impartial and sincere." A mark of the wise is that they don't try to hide their weaknesses.

A year or so later after I visited the team members, I got informed by Jack that many of the angels that were assigned to us had turned. They chose to go to Satan's side. Even the helpers like Andrea and Matt that were made out of our own energy by Father had turned as well. Many people on the team felt hurt and betrayed including myself. I really got to know my angels well and my helpers through out time. If you think about it, Satan chose to not serve Father as well and took many angels with him in the beginning of time. This is why we put our faith and trust in the Lord himself. He may send his angels to help protect us or destroy anything that may be evil or negative, but in reality, he is the only one true God that has created everything. He is our protector, healer, savior, and etc. Once the helpers and angels went over to Satan's side, the Lord created new angels to be put in place to protect his people. Always go with your gut if something feels off.

After graduating high school with my GED and going into my college years, I was learning how to love myself more. I was learning that what you put out into this world, is what you get back. If you put negativity, worry, or fear out there, you will get that back. If you put forth love, healing, and positivity, you will surely get that back as well. Karma is a real honest thing. You can't change anyone but yourself. You are in charge of how to react to your own journey. There are times when the Lord has the right people at the right time come into your life to help you grow into who he needs you to be for Eternity. We all fall short and we all need one another in community. This is why the Lord created us all. We may not all get along or agree with things, but remember that in Eternity, no matter what you have to love your neighbor as you the Lord loves you. That includes yourself. He made us all in his image with all kinds of different personalities. It's truly amazing! I was still in touch with Jack, Linda and Skylar talking to them every now and then. I even went out to visit Michigan a couple more times just to visit and hang out with everyone. They were like my second family from another mother. I loved hanging out with them and being around them.

One day as I sat on the piano at my parents' house my second year of college, I decided to play some worship songs. It was near the winter time so it got dark outside quicker than the summer time. Suddenly, I stopped in the middle of the song and I got up to go to my parents. I turned to my dad and said, "Dad, Nana just died." Nana was my dad's grandma. He looked at me confused and said, "What? How do you know that?" As soon as I was about to respond his phone starts to ring. It was my grandpa telling us the news that Nana had just died. As my dad hung up the phone, he stood their shocked. He couldn't believe how sensitive I was to eternity still.

I really didn't know my Nana that well. I met her once when I was five years old, but other than that I really didn't know much about her. When she passed, she did come to me because I could see her. She was happy and with my Papa in eternity. She did play the Violin at one point in her life when she was fourteen years old just like I played and play now. Nana and Papa were together for over fifty years. They met each other when they were in their young teenage years. My Papa proved his love to my Nana by swimming across the entire lake when he was in his teenage years. It was so sweet.

As time went on, I was still attending the other non-denominational church and going to the New Apostolic Church some of the time. The Lord wanted me to continue his work by helping bring a worship band into his church and honestly go to the New Apostolic Church full time again. The way I woke up to completely leave the non-denominational church was crazy. It will truly blow your mind and it honestly blew mine. The Lord will move you in the right direction of where you need to be no doubt about it.

I was a part of this college youth group at the time with the non-denomination church. We would get together and talk about biblical things in the bible and just be a support group for one another. At the time I thought it was a support group, but I was completely wrong. This lady named Barney at the time was not very nice to me. She didn't include me and got pretty fake with me. Anyway, one night I tried to reach out to her on text message trying to explain to her that my feelings were hurt. She then went off on me and went ballistic to the point of involving a leader from the church to meet us for coffee to get it resolved. I was honestly shocked it went to that point.

We got together that next morning the both of us and our mother and the leader. Right away, Barneys mother had a demon in her space that I noticed. I put up my flowers and I was not ready for what was about to take place. Barney's mother got in my face before I could sit down at the table. She was completely over the top. She was going off on me saying, "Why would you say this to my daughter? Are you crazy?" She was so bad that at one point I literally told her to back off and went crying to the car.

In the car, I balled my eyes out and called my friend Tierra. Tierra was so upset they were acting this way with me when I was just trying to be open and honest about how I felt. It was toxic. My mom didn't run after me either to make sure I was ok. I had no one sticking up for me. I felt truly discouraged and let down.

When I made my way out of the car and back to the table with just enough courage, I went in that ladies' face and I told her to never ever treat me that way again. I don't care who I am, no one deserves that. Her demon and her backed off in that moment. Once she did, Barney and I could actually talk and make peace. She apologized to me and I apologized to her. We were all good and went on our separate ways. I texted my friend Tierra and let her know what happened and that I was ok now. Thankfully everything was over and worked out.

Later on, that night I got ready for bed and got all settled in. I was dead asleep in the middle of the night when my dad lashed into my room. He said, "Olivia! What the heck? Barney's mom is at our door and it's the middle of the night! What did you do now?" Of course, it was always seeming to be my fault so I had to deal with it. Once again, I wasn't stuck up for. I went upstairs terrified for my life as no one in my family cared for my wellbeing. I opened the door shocked. I stood there in my pajamas frightened trying to take deep breaths.

Barney's mom was shaking there standing in anger. I could see the demon in her space raging. I let her cuss me out as I stood there and she threatened my life. She told me, "If I had a gun, I would shoot you." Calling me the evilest person she has ever even met. I asked her what I did. I was confused because I thought we talked later that day in the day time and talked everything out. It was midnight and she was bat shit crazy. She spoke and said, "Your friend Tierra wrote my daughter Barney a nasty message! Look at this!" I looked at her phone and looked at the message my friend Tierra sent. She was expressing to Barney how upset she was with the way I was being treated. At the end of the message my friend Tierra said, "God Bless. I don't want any trouble." I had no clue and tried to explain to Barneys mother that I called Tierra in the car because she was harassing me and I needed someone there for me. I didn't know about Tierra sending any messages.

As Barney's mother walked off, she cussed me out even more saying, "Don't you ever go near us again. You are lucky I didn't kill you or call the police." I went back inside after that just completely shattered. My dad looked at me like I was a complete piece of disappointment and went back to bed. That night I really thought about ending my life. I had an urge to call Linda. As I was shaking trying not to take my own life, Linda picked up on the other end. It was 2am her time in the morning so I was confused as to why she was awake. Linda said, "Olivia, I couldn't sleep all night. I was tossing and turning and I couldn't get to sleep for the life of me. Now I know why. You needed me." I balled to her over the phone telling her how I wanted to end my life because everyone seemed to be against me. She was the only one supporting me. "If that were my house with my child or me, I would have gotten my gun out Olivia. I would have said get off my property." Talking to Linda that night helped save my life.

After that moment happened with those people, my parents made me go to therapy for my problems. They thought that it was me who had the issues. I went to this therapist that they told me to go to and I did. I told the therapist openly and honestly what happened to me and asked what I could do to help change myself. The therapist with years of experience looked at me and said, "You didn't do anything! Who was this lady? I am going to report her. You don't say this to a teenager I don't care who you are." I came home and told my parents what the therapist told me. For some reason, they still didn't stick up for me. Instead, they went to that crazy lazy and her family and begged them for forgiveness for my actions. Why did I want to go to Michigan? Why did I talk to Linda a lot? Because she stood up for me. She knew enough to know the truth of who I am as a person and what the right thing is. She supported me and was there for me to stick up for me.

The last incident that happened to make me leave that non-denominational church was another lady who was supposed to be a girl's only minister in the church. Ministering to the girls of the church and being there for them. Many girls would put their trust and issues in this lady. Confidential things that were private. For me, I reached out to her because other than Linda and Tierra I had no one to talk to about the events that recently happened. Martha was the ladies name who was in charge of this girls only group. I reached out to her because I was having trouble letting go of everything that had happened to me with that lady and then having no support.

I told her all of the things that had happened between Barney and I. How her mother said those horrendous things to me and put me through literal hell and back. I was just trying to speak how I felt I wasn't threatening anyone. I was over people and the church. I was expressing to her all of my frustrations.

Later that day, I get called upstairs by my parents. My dad was furious with me yet again. He hands me these printed out papers of the chat Martha and I had. He yells and says, "What is wrong with you?! Why would you say these things!?" I looked at the messages and in all of the spots that were blank online, Martha herself reworded my words and tried to get that leader in charge Braydon fired. Braydon was one of the youth leaders in the church and also a Pastor. Martha took my words and made it look like I was saying that Braydon was in an inappropriate relationship with Barney.

I started to cry to my dad and say, "I would never do this. I would never say this. You have to believe me." I ran to the computer and frantically looked through my messages with Martha. I yelled, "Look! I told you I didn't say those things." My dad stood over me and saw the real messages. Things I never said only Martha. She tampered with my private messages and sent them over to Braydon. Braydon called us in that day for a meeting with him because he thought I was crazy.

We met up with Braydon and Martha. I was pissed at Martha and I didn't want to see her what so ever. "Why would you do this to a young woman?" said my mom. Martha had nothing to say for herself and just went about her business like she did nothing wrong. She returned to her girls only ministry like nothing had happened. Braydon then banned me from ever joining the worship band at that church again. The Lord sure had his way of giving me a wake-up call.

After all of that, the Lord really opened up my eyes to returning to the New Apostolic Church. This is what I truly believed all along anyway. The other church was corrupt. We may not always get along at church or have tiffs with the people who attend, but it should always be a welcoming place for everyone no matter where you have come from in life. The Lords house is open to all people. I know many people come from different religions and different experiences with different churches and cultures, but the truth is that relationship with the Lord, Jesus, and Holy Spirit is what matters most. The ten commandments are in place because how would you feel if someone did any of those things to you? For example, stealing someone else's things because of jealously or entitlement. It not only hurts the person who is getting stolen from, but it also hurts the stealer in the long run. They have taken something away from someone else that might have meant a lot to them. Another thing that is really important in being a peace maker is to not fight fire with fire. Instead, be kind and be the peace maker.

Chapter 8

T he New Apostolic Church is not heard of much by the world. You many hear more about the Mormon, Catholic, Baptist, Lutheran or the non-denominational church. The New Apostolic Church actually comes from a branch of the Catholic Church. The branch started in England. A group of men challenged the reformation of the Catholic Church back in the 1830's. They wanted to reestablish the Apostle Ministry that Jesus put in place for his people and his church. Back in Jesus time, he established the twelve apostles. The twelve Apostles ordained other people in the Catholic Church to be Apostles as well over time. Eventually, they no longer had Apostles and broke away from that. The men challenging the Catholic Church were just trying to bring back what Jesus had established all along.

The men met together for a year before starting the new church called Catholic Apostolic Church. The Lord chose new Apostles for his people at that point in time and eventually grew to twelve Apostles. They tried going around to other denominations because they did not want to start their own church. The other churches and denominations didn't want anything to do with what they were doing, so they started their own church.

From the 1830's to 1860's, the prophets of the church wanted to expand to have more Apostles for the Lords people.

The Apostles at the time didn't want that to happen and didn't listen to the prophets. It was not of the Lords will to just have twelve Apostles. The Lord wanted there to be more Apostles to grow his work here on earth. Sense the Apostles did not listen, more of the men left that church and created what we have now which is The New Apostolic Church. Jesus brought back the Apostles ministry to prepare for the end time in which we are living now. The church today has expanded to over 10 million people. 8 million of those people live in Africa for The New Apostolic Church. The Lords work has truly grown exceptionally.

Many of the people in the 1980s left a lot of the Denominational churches because of the culture. They didn't like how many would not evolve and change with the times we now live in. For example, many churches today have lively music and worship bands that perform. What many people don't understand is that doctrine is more important than culture is. What you truly believe in has nothing to do with culture. It all has to do with doctrine. The Lord is truly testing his people to see if members will see the importance of the Doctrine instead of the actual culture. I personally realized this when I went from going to a non-denominational church back to the denominational church. The denominational doctrine of the New Apostolic church is what I truly believe because of what I have been through and what I can see in Clairvoyancy.

What is the Doctrine of the New Apostolic Church? This denomination believes in the Father, Son, and Holy Spirit. The foundation was founded on the Bible and the practices of Jesus Christ. They practice the three sacraments which is Holy Baptism, Holy Sealing, and Holy Communion. Baptism with water is the first act of Gods grace in a human believing in Christ. This act is the first step in becoming a true friend of Father, Jesus, and Holy Spirit. Any Priest can bless the water and preform the act of Holy Baptism. In emergency cases, such as being on a death bed, anyone from the church can preform the act. In Holy Sealing, it is performed by an Apostle in prayer and in the form of hands laying on the head. This happens for any Baptized believer and then they become filled with the Holy Spirit and become a child of God.

Every church service we celebrate the sacrament of Holy Communion. This represents the body and blood of Jesus Christ. The mission of the church is to prepare for the return of Jesus. We gather in community in hearing the word of God, worship music and in having Holy Communion. Service for the departed is three times a year on the first Sunday of March, July and November. The New Apostolic Christians pray for the souls who have died in eternity who may be in an unredeemed state. They pray that they may find salvation in Christ. Two ministers receive Holy Baptism with water, Holy Sealing, and Holy Communion on behalf of the dead. The Chef Apostle and the District Apostles give the blessings over the two ministers for this to happen. In other congregations, the departed are prayed for. This takes place after Holy Communion. Before those Sunday services, the members pray for those in eternity that need help and want to come to the service to heal and break free of the sins that may have chained them down.

Many people today get upset with Father because of the chaos and sins of this world. They may say things like, "Why do bad things happen to good people?" The answer is sin. We live in a world full of good and evil combined. It is a world full of sin. No matter how good a person may have been, it all comes back to living in this world and living in sin. This has nothing to do with who you are as a person; it has everything to do with sin.

If you look back to the beginning when Father created the Heavens and the Earth and all of the creatures including Adam and Eve, we see that there was no sin. Everything was perfect in the sight of the Lord. Child birth was painless and there was no pain and suffering. The Lord created Adam and Eve in his imagine just like we all are today. Adam and Eve had authority over all of the animals and creatures the Lord created. The only thing they did not have was to choose to love the Lord or not. Once Eve ate the forbidden apple, sin was created and free will happened.

The Lord allowed this to happen because without free will, we wouldn't have the opportunities that we do now to love the Lord because we truly want to. Wanting to grow in relationship with our creator and willingly choose be a part of Fathers life is an amazing gift. Plus, the Lord wants his people to be able to come to him and not be mindless drones. He wants a true real relationship with us. Just like when it comes to relationships with other people. Wouldn't we want the real thing? I wouldn't want a fake relationship. Unfortunately, until Jesus comes, we do live in this sinful good and evil world that is filled with pain and sorrow. It is what it is.

Another thing to think about is who we are as people. Our ancestors went through so much for us and our families that we have now today. They suffered a great deal so our family and their family could be where we are at today. We would not be here today if it were not for them. That is why the Lord pronounces that we respect our elders and our ancestors. In doing this, we need to also respect our bodies and treat that as a temple. We come from our ancestors and we come from the Lord. We were created in the imagine of the Lord so we must be grateful and we must treat our bodies like temples and love ourselves. When I say love yourself, I mean love yourself as the Lord loves you and not in an egoistic way.

Coming back into the New Apostolic Church was refreshing for me after being at the other non-denominal church. I had nothing against them at all, it just wasn't what I believed in. The only thing I honestly liked was the worship music. They had huge bands and instruments which was amazing.

When I came back into the church, I wanted to join the choir. I loved to sing so I decided that's where I would be best. At the time, the church was still opening up to the ideas of growing and changing to become more modern. Of course, still keeping the doctrine of the church, but just trying to change the culture a bit.

In the year of 2013 shortly after I left the non-denominational church, I decided to possibly try to start a worship band at the church. This was a big jump and a huge leap of faith because the church just had orchestra and choir at the time. I got together a group of people who were interested in trying something different. We had some members as well that were very excited and wanted to use their gifts for the Lord in playing the drums, guitar, and etc. I was truly excited and ready to put together this band for the Lord work. We always practiced very hard and always had the reminder to worship the Lord. It wasn't a performance; it was worship.

Over time, some of the members did not like the change in the music. We had some back lash at times, but everyone is different. I liked how we now had a variety of modern music and old school as well. It was a good variation of everything and it made worship really exciting. We had a good run of things for awhile until ego seemed to take a big play in things. People were starting to want what they wanted and treated it more like a spot light instead of worship. When you allow that kind of spirit into the work of the Lord it will fail every time. Eventually, people that were apart of the band just started to drop out. It became what it was which is choir and orchestra. It was the Lords test of faith to us if we would stay in the church for the doctrine and not just the culture because doctrine is more important than any culture. It is what you truly believe.

Living in what we call the end time now, the church is preparing the Lords people for the return of Jesus. No one knows when Jesus will return to take us home to Heaven for the wedding feast, but we still prepare by being ourselves and having that true relationship with Father, Jesus and Holy spirit. The true keys to unlocking healing, love and becoming more like Jesus is to just look inward. Most of the time, we are just standing in our own way. Here on this earth, we need to go through the lessons of life. There is no failing, just learning. If you mess something up or come to find that you don't like something, you learn to not go through it again. This is the Lord preparing us for the return of Jesus. This life on earth isn't easy, but its also not eternity in Heaven.

Before the day of the Lord is to come, there are seven stages of what we call the seven scrolls. Many people believe the scrolls to be stages throughout time itself. We are warned of what is to come and what to prepare for through the book of Revelations. There are still many mysteries we may not know or understand of with earth and our universe. In time we will come to find the answers only through the Lord. He knows what we can and can't handle.

The first scroll indicates a rider going out on a white horse and he claims a bow, but no mention of arrows. This is a sign of military power. The rider itself is an indication of the anti-Christ who will deceive the world into believing him to be the savior. He will mimic Christ, who will also be riding a white horse at his coming. The symbol of having no arrows could mean the anti-Christ as to being a fake peace marker. Later he will bring war.

This second scroll is taking more about war with the anti-Christ being in charge. The red horse represents the blood and anger. Matthew 24:7 "Nation will rise against nation and kingdom against kingdom." The anti-Christ will gain leadership and corrupt the world.

The black horse and the rider that holds the pair of scales represents famine for the third scroll. There will be a lack of food from the wars and nuclear weapon fall out. Many places all over the world will have to rise prices due to the lack of food supply. This is also a sign of control coming from the anti-Christ. It is a way to enforce the mark of the beast. The scales also represent a weighing of food so you wouldn't be able to take much. There will also be great earth quakes on earth.

A pale horse named Death and having hades follow represented the fourth scroll. They were given power over a fourth of the earth to kill by sword, meaning famine, plague and etc. The Lord warned his people that if they were not faithful to him, he would allow and release the four categories. Many believed that the fourth seal happened near the fourteenth century.

In the fifth scroll, it indicated those asking the Lord how much longer until he judges the earth. They were told a little while longer and given a white robe. These were the people who were greatly wronged by people who might have been murders, stealers, or etc. This was said to be spoken by people in eternity.

Earth quakes, the sun turning black, the moon turning red, and the mountains and islands disappearing indicates the sixth scroll. The final seventh scroll indicates having a brief pause and silence in Heaven. The following will be judgements and who comes to the wedding feast and who stays in the chaos on earth.

When the day comes for Jesus to take us home, he will firstly take all of those in eternity and then come for the people on earth. The people who have no relationship with Father, Jesus, and Holy Spirit will be left in the chaos that will occur on earth. As well as anyone who as not believed in him. We need to be able to change our ways of sin and become more Christ like. Its not going to be easy, it's a hard tough road, but in the end, it is worth it. In the end, everything is truly in the hands of Jesus if you are taken or not. The day of the Lord will come like a thief in the night. Once Jesus has taken those to go with him, the angels that are holding up the four corners of the earth will let go. They will let go of the sheets of peace, love, joy, light, and etc. that would have been held over the earth.

Once that has been completed the angels that held up the four corners of the earth will attend the chaos back down on earth. People will be screaming and running up to them asking for help. The angels will not know what they mean because they will have no emotion. They will not know what emotion means. There will be a great earth quake and the sun will become black. The moon will turn blood red. It will truly be Hell on earth and Satan's playground. All of the demons will be unleashed from Hell and make the world what they want it to be. There will be no peace, love, anything that Father has given us now.

The wedding feast will be held in Heaven for three and a half years. This will conclude with Jesus choosing the Bride of Christ out of the Lords children (A child of God). Everyone will celebrate and enjoy being in eternity and Heaven. There will be no sin so no stealing, murdering, etc. We will get to know our ancestors and all of the people who have walked before us in time. There will be no time, just eternity.

After the wedding feast, there will be a thousand years of peace where Satan will be locked away where he will no longer be able to influence evil in any kind of way to the Lords people. There will be no suffering from evil or wickedness. The people who were at the wedding feast will come down to earth to preach the good news of Jesus to the people who were stuck in the chaos on earth. Some of the people will reject Jesus from the pain and suffering they had to suffer from the chaos on earth. The people coming down from Heaven from the wedding feast will come down to spread the word of the Lord so everyone will know of Jesus and know the truth of his word and ways.

Once the thousand years of peace are over, Satan will be released into the world once more and he will try to convince everyone against the Lord, Jesus and Holy Spirit. He will try to make people believe in him and his ways, but in all reality, he just wants everyone to die with him when he gets thrown into the lake of fire. Satan will be released for a short period of time. We don't know how much period of time that will be.

Judgement day will come once the short period for Satan is over. Judgement will render on everyone who has ever lived by Jesus. From this time and day forward, this is when Jesus will choose who stays with Father, Jesus and Holy Spirit with them forever in eternity. The people who choose to go with Satan, will be thrown into the lake of fire with him. The lake of fire is not hell or torment. You are destroyed forever permanently. There will no longer be Satan or demons and your soul is completely destroyed forever.

The new heaven and the new earth are created after judgement day. The people who have chosen Father, Jesus, and Holy Spirit will live with them forever eternally in the new heaven and the new earth. There will be no more tears of pain, suffering, fear, and etc. It will be everything of the light that Father, Jesus and Holy Spirit have. Love will radiant throughout the new heaven and new earth onto all of the Lords people.

Chapter 9

During my later teenage years and into my college years, I focused on myself and how I could help further the Lords work for his people. I learned many things including to always work on myself first before helping other people. If you don't care for yourself, there is no possible way to help other people. Another thing that I have learned is being cautious. If you have the gift to be able to see things or feel things, be cautious as to who you are seeing or feeling. Thing will not always be as they seem. Satan likes to try to fake people or lead people the wrong way. Always one hundred percent trust your gut. Your gut instinct comes from your third charka and it will always be honest with you. If something doesn't feel right or something is off, do not trust that. Even if you are seeing someone clairvoyantly and they are telling you that they are something they may not be, trust your gut.

Your third eye or sixth charka is where clairvoyant people can see things such as souls who have passed, angels, auras, and etc. This is also the area of which you create your world within yourself and how you see yourself in each charka. This is where you truly figure out yourself and all of the things you may or may not be dealing with. People call this looking inward with meditation. In the sixth charka you can create your own home. Some people just create where they feel most comfortable like the beach or a childhood home or memory. It can be anywhere you would feel at home.

I had a few moments when I would meditate and I would see different things at different times. One of the experiences that I remember well was speaking to the Lord and Jesus. I was walking through a garden with a lot of fog. It was hard to see at times and not much was growing on the ground. It was more of a dirt and some what green grass path. I walked over with Jesus to one of the trees he was showing me. The tree looked like a weeping willow tree without any leaves. It was starved of water and looking like it may collapse at any moment. It was very brittle and weak. On the other side of the tree next to the pathway, was a tree that was flourishing with many kinds of fruits and bright green tree leaves. It was strong and sturdy and filled with a lot of nutrients and hydration. Jesus pointed to the tree that was weak and brittle. He said, "This is the tree of death." Names started to appear on the tree that I couldn't make out like post it notes. "Many people who have no relationship with me or Father are on this tree of death. It has no life." He pointed to the next tree which was flourishing. "This tree is the tree of life. Anyone who has believed in me and has a relationship has the tree of life." Names appeared on this tree as well like sticky notes. He pointed one more time to show me my name on the tree of life. He smiled and gave me a loving hug.

The final vision I remember having was being in a place I had never been before. I remember going up to this big castle that was super peaceful. Inside there were many book shelves and a nice big fire place. I saw a nice rocking chair in the middle of the room with a nice coffee table. Everything looked like it was fit for a king in this place. I couldn't see the Lord, but I felt like he was there in the rocking chair rocking back and forth wearing some reading glasses. The Lord does not need glasses, but I felt like he wore them for humor. The Lord is very sarcastic and we shoot a lot of jokes back and forth with one another. He was sitting in the chair looking into this book and he was writing things in it almost like a story.

I went outside to look at the yard and it was amazing. The pavement was laid out in nice stone that looked rustic. There were little gardens everywhere and it was just a peace I couldn't describe. I sat at this picnic table that was pure white outside on the pavement. It was beautiful. Jesus came over in his white robe and sat next to me. I asked, "What is this place?" He looked over the gardens and said, "In time, you will know." As he smiled, we just sat and talked about life. Suddenly, in the garden a bit in the distance I saw a white horse. It was almost as white as light. I feel like that represented Jesus and him coming soon when I saw the white horse.

One of the fun things that I didn't realize I did until recently is pulling up energy. When ever the stove would be heating up very slowly and I would be standing there waiting for it to work, I would put my hand over the stove and pull on the energy. I don't know how, but I would pull up the heat quicker than it would load onto the stove itself. I would also do this with the water for the bath or faucet. Sometimes, the water or stove would only get so hot because the utility itself wouldn't allow it to get that hot or warm. I laugh about it today wondering why I do that anyway. I also try to do this with things that don't work as they should. It's a very strange thing, but at times it seems to work.

After I had the visions I had of the garden and the castle, we had service for the departed on that following Sunday. I went to church that morning and remember sitting by myself in the pew. It was a good service about praying for those in the departed and loving one another as the Lord loves us. As I was sitting there, I felt my brother Andy next to me. He was holding a baby in his arms. There was a couple from the church that just had a miscarriage recently. They were hurting and very heart broken. My brother held the baby in his arms with his thumbs up indicating that the baby was ok. I went to the couple after church service and pulled them aside to tell them. They were blown away, but also thankful. Hearing any message from eternity is a blessing and creates peace for us here on earth.

When children are miscarried or aborted, in eternity they go to a place where people can teach them about Jesus and the faith. To me it almost looks like a hospital on earth. They get taught and taken care of by the people of that realm that are helping those souls. My brother was actually one of those people that helps out in that realm. There are many kinds of realms that I spoke about early that people can go to. Most of the people from the realm of paradise go out and help other souls that are in darker realms. I'll never forget my cousin's grandpa telling us about how everything in eternity was on the outside. If you had a broken heart, or a bullet to the head, in eternity everyone could see that. You could not hide anything you were dealing with, including sin.

The very next Sunday that year I was attending church like normal. I was just sitting there listening to service to hear the word of the Lord from the person who was speaking. I always see a bright white light behind who ever is serving. That bright light is the Holy Spirit. Sometimes it is so bright that it actually hurts my eyes if I am looking in that direction for too long. Its so powerful that my focus doesn't just go to the person who is serving, but the words that are coming out of the servant directly from the Holy Spirit. As I was sitting there, I saw a man who was sitting above us all. A lot of eternity during services either sits by you, or they sit above everyone who is on earth for the service. I saw the man sitting in a spot with chains on his wrists. He was chained down with tears in his eyes. He looked so tired and terrified as he brushed his black long curly hair away from his face. He looked back at me and smiled and I said, "Who are you? You look familiar." He spoke and said, "I'm Michael Jackson." I looked at him and smiled and told him I would pray for him. I haven't seen him sense that day, but it's important to pray for everyone here on earth and in eternity.

A part of the bible that was actually taken out of most bibles was called the Apocrypha. It is only in a few bibles now including the New Apostolic Church. It has some pretty amazing facts in there. One of my favorites that my grandpa actually spoke to us about is the seven stages you go through after you pass away. In summary, the first stage occurs when the person who has passed has served Father, Jesus and Holy Spirit despite any hardship and followed the lawgiver of the land. They see the glory of the Lord and are accepted by the Lord. Then they enter into a period of rest. Their first joy is victory from their long fight in their sin and human bodies.

The second stage which is called the second joy is seeing punishment for the wicked and evil. Jumping into the third stage of joy, the Lord gives them good report so that they kept the law and kept that entrusted. The fourth stage of joy is interesting. They go into storehouses in eternity to learn the rest of which is kept secret and are guarded by angels in deep silence. In there, they may learn much more about eternity than we do here on earth. Some of the things that they would know or learn in that storehouse or eternity itself might be too much for us here on earth. It would be too much for our earthly bodies to handle to know everything. There is glory waiting for them in the next stage of life for them which is eternity.

In the fifth stage of joy, the person who has passed gets to see the earth on which they have escaped from the sin and corruption. They get to see and understand the life of eternity for eternal life. They are to shine like the stars never to fade or die in the sixth stage of joy. The final last stage is them receiving their reward in glory. They are free from fear, shame and get to see the Lord. You can find exactly what it says in Esdras 2:7 verses 88-101.

My grandpa on my moms' side of the family passed away in 2015. Before he passed, the Lord came to me in a vision and told me that he was going to pass soon. I didn't know how long soon meant, but we were all very close to him. It was hard at first to hear that, but I know he is in a good place and helping many souls. He's just on a new journey now. When people pass, they can see everyone's energy and thoughts. Nothing is hidden and everything is revealed. Its like when someone takes their clothes off, you never know what's under there.

After the Lord told me about my grandpas passing, I told my parents so they would know and prepare. It was so hard for us, but we cherished each and every moment we had. He didn't pass until three years after the Lord told me that he would. The Lords timing is so different from our own. To him soon could mean tomorrow or years. For us we think soon as in a couple of hours, days or even weeks. Eternity has no time so things go by differently there than it is here on earth. My grandpa could still see us and be by us when he passed. It wasn't until the day of his funeral when he went to eternity to where he needed to go. They do not leave until the Priest who is holding the funeral services says the final words of ashes to ashes and dust to dust.

Before my grandpa's funeral took place, he would be amazed at eternity and energy not being in a physical body anymore. He would travel between my grandma and all of the family members to comfort us. He knew that I could see him so he would play little tricks. I would be walking in my grandmas living room and I would feel a physical pull to the point of like someone poked my side and pushed me a little. My grandpa would laugh like a big kid and say, "Wow this is neat!" He would also turn on sinks out of the blue and make sure we knew he was around us. He was a hoot.

Some people can move objects after they pass away if they are strong enough to do so. Other people can not do this and don't have enough strength. After the funeral, my grandpa went to where he needed to be and was greeted by many ancestors in eternity. He went on to help souls in the dark realms to spread the word of the gospel to those who needed help. He would also invite them to services to help free them from the dark realms or chains they were bearing. Other people can actually become stuck here on earth trapped by their bodies of where they passed away. They get stuck because of unforgiveness or anger, but eventually get taken to where they need to be in eternity.

My grandpa passed in a very peaceful way. He had many health problems through out his life, but he was a true faithful servant of the Lord. He went to the hospital one night because he was having some unusual acid reflex and chest pain. He checked into the hospital and they kept him over night. They ran all kinds of tests on him to make sure everything was ok and the doctor told him that he was completely fine. He was in the room with the doctor and nurses right as he just passed out dead. When the Lord calls you home and takes your soul out of the body, there is no reviving the body.

When souls pass away, they have no gender. The Lord created the human body which does have gender, but the soul which is made up of energy does not. This is why we have so many people who change genders or feel like they should be something else it is because the Lord created the soul that has no gender. The Lord created you and your personality in the way he did. If you choose to be a man, woman, or etc. it really doesn't matter. He loves us all unconditionally and this is the way he created us. The Lord calls us to love one another no matter what gender because love is love.

When our loved ones pass away, they will come to us as we would feel comfortable. For example, my grandpa comes to me as he was when he passed so I don't freak out and say, "Who the heck are you?!" They do this so you don't feel freaked out by their true soul and energy that they become in eternity. I truly have no clue what that truly looks like, but one day we will all know. It's too much for our human bodies to handle what actually truly occurs in eternity. It is a whole different dimension to the next stage of life.

There is no need to worry or be anxious about anything in this life. We all live and we all pass away. Everything is truly in the Lords hands and he has each and every one of us here on this earth for a reason. He created each and every one of us in his image. We all may be different or come from different places in life, but we are all made to live life together. To forgive and to love just as the Lord loves us. It's not easy by any means, but in eternity, we will all be together and stand before the almighty creator, Jesus and Holy Spirit. He made us to help one another and need one another because we are all in the same boat.

The heart needs the organs to survive as well as water. We need nutrients and different components for our body to survive. Just like we need each other. The Lord created us to live as one in all of our various talents and gifts he gave us. If we can't get along or accept one another for who we truly are in all of our personalities, gifts and talents, where will we be? Ego, jealousy, and anything that is not of the Lord has no place in the kingdom of Heaven. We truly have to work inward with ourselves and understand our own blockages that can cause us to tend to be in the way of all of our sinful nature. It is important to understand and heal within.

With the gift that clairvoyancy brings, it can be challenging. The Lord created each and every one of us different. Not everyone can handle seeing and feeling things in the other dimension. It is not for the faint of heart and takes a much greater understanding of that world. If you may see things or feel them, you have to know the truth of eternity. You have to protect yourself and gain the knowledge and wisdom that comes with the gift. It's not a game. You have to learn how to handle it responsibility or you invite Satan's crap into your life. When you invite the crap of Satan, it will destroy you. Go by the bible and what the bible says. The Lord has the bible for that purpose, to lead and guide us all in the truth. If you do not see things or feel them, do not try to use things to call on the dead or do things to what you want. It welcomes spirits and demons into the home and you put yourself in danger as well as others. Even if you do see, never call on anything. At the right time, the Lord will choose what happens and what he wants to reveal for you.

Through all of my experiences and all of the things I have learned, I'm grateful to have learned what I have learned. Every single day is a chance to become better within yourself. To love and forgive others is also so important not only for your sake, but also for others as well. Bitterness creates health issues and lots of trauma to the soul. Doing this to yourself not only hurts yourself, but this hurts other too. Don't allow yourself to be chained to sin, allow yourself to be set free. The healing begins from going within.

9 781638 377191